FOR INSTRUCTION AND RECREATION

The Museum
York

Dear Sir

The Council of the Yorkshire Philosophical
Society invites you to attend a meeting of Curators
of provincial Museums to consider the following
points —.
(1) The desirability of forming a Museum Association
(2) The constitution and government of such
Association
(3) A few of the more important objects which
such an Association should keep in view

Three dates are suggested for this meeting —
May 2nd 3rd 4th and it is intended to fix upon
that day which is most convenient to the majority
of those invited. Would you kindly let me
know _before_ April 20th if you have any preference, and if so, which day will suit you best.

April 12th 1888.   Yours faithfully
                              H. M. Platnauer

W. W. Midgley. Esq.

FRONTISPIECE: The follow-up letter calling the meeting which led to the
formation of the Museums Association. It is addressed to W W Midgley, Curator
of the Chadwick Museum, Queen's Park, Bolton.

FOR INSTRUCTION AND RECREATION

A Centenary History of the Museums Association

Geoffrey Lewis

Quiller Press
London

The Museums Association gratefully acknowledges the financial
support of the Carnegie United Kingdom Trust towards the
publication of this centenary history.

First published by
Quiller Press Ltd
46 Lillie Road, London SW6 1TN

ISBN 1-870948-37-8

Design by Jim Reader

Design and production in association with
Book Production Consultants, Cambridge

Typesetting services by Cambridge Photosetting Services

Printed and bound in Great Britain by
The Burlington Press, Foxton, Cambridge

CONTENTS

PREFACE

This volume is intended to fulfil two needs. The first is to mark the centenary of the Museums Association and place on record some of the Association's many achievements, some of which were made against considerable difficulties. The second follows from the first. Because the Association has been closely associated with so many of the key events in museum development during the last century, it provides an opportunity to link these with some of the contemporary professional literature. For this reason the events have been closely referenced to provide a supporting bibliography. Neither of these goals, however, could be met comprehensively, because of the limitations of time and space.

I would like to thank the Museums Association for inviting me to pen its official history and the University of Leicester for the time to write it during my last term before retirement. Many people have helped to make the work possible, too many to name individually. However, particular mention should be made of Graeme Farnell and Jane Swinton at the Association for their help with sources. I am also grateful to Lynne Teather of the Museum Studies Program at the University of Toronto for the copy of an index of the *Museums Journal* which she kindly made available to me. By no means last, my thanks to Frances, my wife, who shared the same periods of solitude to see the work through.

Wolvey, July 1989   Geoffrey Lewis

CHAPTER ONE

PRELUDE

The Museums Association had a gestation period of over a decade. It started at a time when museums, particularly those in the provinces, were the butt of much criticism. The correspondence columns of the periodical *Nature* carried some of this criticism during the summer of 1877 under the heading 'Museum Reform'. But the catalyst for this seems to have been an address given to the Manchester Literary and Philosophical Society by Professor W Boyd Dawkins (1876), Curator of the Manchester Museum at Owen's College. In it he adversely compared the museums of Britain with those he had visited abroad which, he claimed, 'were as a rule well officered, well arranged and not dependent on private resources for their sustenance'. In Britain, he said, 'a museum is a sort of advertising bazaar, or a receptacle for miscellaneous curiosities unfitted for a private house, or it is composed of an accumulation of objects, valuable in themselves but valueless for all practical purposes, because they are crowded together or stowed away for want of room'. It is clear from Professor Boyd Dawkins' remarks that his concern and criticism was directed primarily at the private and society institutions which then comprised the majority of the country's museums.

At this time about forty museums were supported from the rate funds of the municipalities. This had become possible, initially through the *Museums Act 1845* and, from 1850, mainly by public library legislation; the Free Public Museum at Liverpool, however, had been established in 1852 as a result of a local act of parliament. Most of these municipal museums had been built around existing collections, many of them from the learned societies whose museums were now the subject of some criticism. In addition, the number of museums was increasing rapidly: from about ninety in 1860, the number had doubled by 1880. Many of these new museums were created by local authorities in response to civic pride or to ensure continuity of previous privately owned collections. The result was often a heterogeneous collection of great curiosity but little educational value.

Under the enabling legislation for municipal libraries and museums the expenditure could not exceed a one-penny rate and this was a major restraint in providing these services. Although attempts had been made in parliament to raise the rate level, this was not to be achieved generally for these dual but distinctive functions during the nineteenth century. Among those active in improving the financial position of libraries and museums was Anthony John Mundella, the Radical member of parliament for Sheffield. Another matter of concern was the failure of the Royal Commission for the Exhibition of 1851 to make available some of its surplus funds for the benefit of provincial museums. It had contributed to the formation of the South Kensington Museum. In January 1887 a meeting of municipal authorities with museum responsibilities was held in Birmingham to urge their claim but without success; it was argued that much of the fund had been derived from provincial sources. This meeting also discussed the duplicates held by the State museums and the desirability of provincial museums being able to show them. Subsequently Mundella, with Joseph Chamberlain who represented Birmingham, proposed amendments to the British Museum legislation to promote the gift of duplicate specimens to provincial museums.

Of the government-funded museums in London, the British Museum had already been in existence for over a century and, despite having been completely re-built, was suffering from severe over-crowding. Now, in contradiction both of the findings of a select committee of the House of Commons and of the Trustees of the Museum, the government had decided to erect a separate building at South Kensington to house the natural history collections. As a consequence of this transfer, the rooms left vacant at Bloomsbury by the geology and mineralogy collections were being redeployed by the Greek and Roman Department while the space occupied by Botany provided much needed accommodation for the British and Medieval Department.

At South Kensington the Museum, opened under the Government's Department of Science and Art in 1857, had by now been a public facility for twenty years. Created as a centre for consulting the best works of art and science and intended to influence and improve industrial design in the nation, the South Kensington Museum had already been the subject of considerable enlargement and now was currently drawing up the specifications for a new art library. In May 1876 Queen Victoria had opened a major loan exhibition of scientific apparatus to which several European countries and the United States had contributed; some examples of applied science were also exhibited. A number of these objects were incorporated into the Museum's science collections at the close of the exhibition. Associated with the exhibition, Professor W H Flower (1876) delivered a summer lecture on 'Museum specimens for teaching purposes' and this was serialized in *Nature* a few months later.

It was in response to articles by Professors Flower and Boyd Dawkins that the idea of a Museums Association is first mooted. Elijah Howarth,

FIG. 2: Elijah Howarth, Curator of the Weston
Park Museum, Sheffield.

recently appointed Curator of the Weston Park
Museum at Sheffield, wrote to *Nature* in
January 1877 suggesting to those responsible
for the management of museums that
mutual co-operation would assist in
developing their full potential. He does
not elaborate in detail on the particular
issues for mutual co-operation but there
can be little doubt that they included:
the inadequate funding of museums;
their educational potential, particularly
in relation to the recent elementary
education acts; the need for provincial
museums to have clear aims and for
curators 'to content themselves with
doing only what can be done thoroughly
and well . . . and not to accept objects
simply with a view to filling empty cases'.

The idea of an association to foster
co-operation among colleagues was hardly
novel. A number of professional groups
– engineers, meteorologists, veterinary
surgeons, for example – had recently formed
associations and the librarians were to
establish one later in 1877. However,
there was no immediate response to Howarth's
call. Instead the correspondence columns of
Nature concentrated, as far as museums were concerned, on the general
need for reform. Following a further article by Boyd Dawkins (1877) in
which he particularly criticizes the lack of order in many museum displays,
he then adds that some museums are visited as places of amusement, where
'a happy day' may be spent, rather than as places of instruction. They are
'sometimes avowedly arranged for that end'. The need for museum reform
is then developed by F W Rudler (1877), then a lecturer in natural science at
Aberystwyth but who became Curator of the Museum of Practical
Geology in London. He viewed museums as 'educational engines' and
called for museums to restrict their aims. Many museums, he stated, 'teach
too little by attempting to teach too much.' About the same time he was
campaigning for a central museum of natural history in Wales (Bassett 1982).

It is at this point that a further provincial museum curator enters
the debate. James Paton (1877), appointed Curator of the Kelvingrove
Museum, Glasgow the previous year, confesses that much of what Boyd

3

Dawkins describes is true. However, he says, 'a specialist, though an indispensable cultivator of science, is a very bad museum curator' who, rather, should be like 'a newspaper editor, a man of general knowledge and culture' and with 'an experimental knowledge of the routine duties of a museum, such as can only be obtained by training . . .'. Paton then develops the need for training curators, for finance, for a public appreciation of the nature and functions of museums, for the improvement of labels and the development of an exchange programme for duplicate specimens between museums. Vast good would result, he said, from a conference of museum keepers; whether this was an endorsement of Howarth's suggestion some seven months earlier or an independent proposal is not clear; certainly Howarth and Paton were known to each other, having met in Glasgow the previous year. All of the personalities involved in this *Nature* correspondence were, over a decade later, to play a part in the formation or development of the Museums Association. For the time being, however, except for a letter of support from the Director of the Royal Zoological, Anthropological and Ethnographical Museum in Dresden, Dr A B Meyer (1877), the matter rested for nearly three years.

In March 1880, James Paton (1880a) wrote to the Editor of *Nature* again: 'I desire now to see some effort made to bring the question to a practical issue [and] with this in view I shall be glad to co-operate with other museum officials who feel inclined to take part in the organizing of a conference'. There were further letters, but not from the provincial museum officials to whom it had been directed. The first discordant note also appears. A contributor, writing under the pseudonym 'Academicus' (1880), deprecated most strongly any attempt to form an association to talk about museums, claiming that proper salaries for curators were the answer to the museums' problems and that these would ensure that the curator attended during office hours rather than 'lecturing here or there and eking out his pay by literature'. This brought an immediate rejoinder from James Paton (1880b) and also from J Romilly Allen (1880a,b), later Editor of *The Reliquary*, who had already indicated his support and now proposed that the subject should be brought forward at the next meeting of the British Association for the Advancement of Science in York. At the same time James Paton announced that the Council of the Royal Society of Arts would give the proposed conference their support if an executive committee was formed for the purpose. These interventions were important because the cause was no longer identified with the natural scientists alone. Support also came from another source, Edward Morell Holmes (1880), Curator of the Pharmaceutical Society's museums in London, who strongly supported an early response to the offer of the Royal Society of Arts.

But for reasons which appear to have been a lack of interest among provincial museum officials, the projected meeting did not materialize. This does not mean that any discussion of museums and their problems was dead. Indeed, the President of the Biology Section of the British

Association for the Advancement of Science chose to give his address on 'Museums, their Use and Improvement' in that year and apart from publication in the Report of the Association, it also appeared in *Nature*. As Keeper of the Department of Zoology at the British Museum, Dr A C G Günter (1880) understandably devoted some of his attention to the current move of the natural science collections from Bloomsbury to South Kensington. However, apart from national museums he also spoke on two other classes of museum: provincial and educational. 'The principal aim of a provincial museum ought, in my opinion, to be popular instruction,' said Dr Günter. He did not see them merely as a place for mild amusement and recreation but equal with other institutions which spread knowledge and cultivate taste. On the question of the British Museum supplying duplicate specimens to the provincial museums, he expressed the view that a curator who has to be satisfied with the mechanical work of displaying and preserving objects acquired, which are prepared and named for him by others, takes less interest in the progress of his museum than one who has to form a collection.

Four years later, we find Elijah Howarth attending the Dublin meeting of the Library Association at the request of several people anxious to find a forum for museum officials. This may be regarded as surprising for although the posts of librarian and curator were frequently combined, the arrangement was rarely satisfactory for the museum as the British Association (1887) was to report three years later. However, while the annual meeting of the Library Association appeared to receive the suggestion favourably, its Council decided that it did not wish to extend the Association's area of operation. The Library Association was in its early days dominated by librarians from the state, university and private sector (Kelly, 1977) and this may, in itself, have been a reason for the failure of a proposal from a group of municipal museum curators.

The 1880s saw a marked increase in the number of municipal museums. Among the major local authorities now providing them were Birmingham, Bootle, Brighton, Leeds, Manchester (Queen's Park), Oldham, Reading and Wolverhampton. This inevitably provided an additional impetus to form an Association, as did the introduction of new approaches and techniques. One innovation was the introduction by Liverpool in 1884 of its 'Circulating School Museum' which may be regarded as the beginning of school loans services in Britain. The same Museum was also examining its clientele and had come to the conclusion that some 78% of its visitors come without any clearer purpose than to see the museum while 20% were children or 'loungers'; the remainder were considered to be serious students. The Revd Henry Higgins (1885), who reported this in a paper to the Literary and Philosophical Society of Liverpool in 1885, went on to say that he would regard a donation of £100 for the museum best spent on making the order of the Museum more intelligible and instructive rather than purchasing new specimens.

The concern to improve the provincial museums and understand their problems led to the creation in 1886 of a Committee on Provincial Museums by the British Association for the Advancement of Science; they were allocated £5 for the work. Following a survey, which included all the municipal boroughs in the United Kingdom, the Committee produced its first report in 1887. The enquiry embraced all museums out of London to which the public could obtain access and the report lists 211 of these. About one-half had originated as local society museums while one-quarter commenced as private collections. By the time of the report (British Association, 1887), one half of the society museums had been transferred either to municipal corporations or to trustees for the public benefit. Only a dozen of the private collections were still in private hands. The report provides important data on a wide variety of aspects of the museum operation and curatorial practice. Several of the respondents emphasized the importance of museums being controlled by scientific curators rather than town councils or amateurs. Several others felt the need for an organization among curators to facilitate mutual help and co-operation.

The following year this Committee reported on the ideal to which the fast increasing municipal rate-supported free museums should aspire with suggestions on how to approach such an ideal (British Association 1888). Beyond the preservation and display of specimens, the special aims of such a museum were seen firstly to contribute to the scientific knowledge of the country by collecting from its locality and to receive and preserve local collections and specimens of scientific value offered for public use. From these, the report said, displays should provide the greatest amount of popular instruction consistent with the preservation of the specimens and their accessibility for study, to which other specimens, to demonstrate scientific principles or relationships between the locality and the rest of the world, might be added. Following a number of practical recommendations the report concluded:

> The practical value of museums as important factors in all adequate systems of education is not yet recognized by the general public. Too many of these institutions have hitherto been but toys and hobbies, and require complete re-organisation. We are not aware of a single free rate-supported provincial museum in the kingdom which has attained the ideal recommended in this report.

The British Association's study had confirmed an interest in forming an organization among curators. It now remained for a meeting to be called to progress the idea. This was undertaken by the Yorkshire Philosophical Society. The Society's Council minutes record that Henry Platnauer, the Keeper of its Museum, was given permission to write to other curators for this purpose (Pyrah, 1988) implying that the actual request came from Platnauer. Wherever the initiative occurred, a letter signed by Platnauer was sent on Leap Year Day 1888 from the Museum at York to twenty-four of the 'best-known' English museums assessing interest in a conference to form a museums association. The response being positive, further letters were sent giving an option of dates in May and then confirming the meeting for the afternoon of 3 May 1888 (see frontispiece). Eleven persons[1] representing nine provincial museums met in the house of the Vice-President of the Yorkshire Philosophical Society, S W North, who chaired the meeting.

The meeting discussed a number of issues of professional concern including the interchange of duplicate specimens, the need for a concerted effort to obtain Government publications, the issue of a journal, the indexing of the general contents of museums and the sharing of practical experience, particularly concerning the arrangement and classification of specimens. Finally it was agreed unanimously that a Museums Association be formed consisting of curators and those engaged in the active work of museums and also of representatives of the committees or councils of management of such museums. It was also suggested that the proposed Association publish a volume of practical papers, and if possible scientific contributions, and also arrange periodic meetings, at least annually. It was agreed that details of the meeting should be sent to all provincial museums in England.

Two issues are worthy of note at this stage. The first is that the initial invitation and that for the inaugural meeting was restricted to English museums only. Nowhere in the bland minutes of the day is any reason given for this. However, it did mean that one of the principal early protagonists for an association, James Paton, Curator of the Kelvingrove Museum in Glasgow, did not participate in the founding work. The other factor, however, has had a lasting effect on the Association over the century of its existence and has been a matter of debate on a number of occasions. This was the proposed inclusion of representatives of museum committees within the Association. In this, the Museums Association followed closely the model of the Library Association but as to the reasons for it the record is silent; it may have been simple financial expediency or a more profound reason. The proposed realization of the Association, however, was now different from 'an association of curators and others engaged in the arrangement of museums' or a 'conference of museum keepers' as envisaged by Elijah Howarth and James Paton respectively some eleven years previously.

CHAPTER TWO

BEGINNINGS

The inaugural meeting of the Museums Association was held on 20 June 1889 in York at the invitation of the Council of the Yorkshire Philosophical Society. As one of the foremost of the country's provincial learned societies with its own fine museum in the care of a paid curator, the venue was an attractive one. Further the Society had played host in 1831 to the founding meeting of another organization, the now highly successful and popular British Association for the Advancement of Science. The circular calling the meeting embodied an account of the initial meeting of the previous year, listed some of the advantages that co-operation could bring and suggested that it could connect together naturalists in the Kingdom. As resolved by that meeting, it was sent to all English provincial museums. It suggested that each museum might send its curator and two or more members of its governing body to the meeting. The list in the British Association (1887) report was used for the invitations; it names 159 such museums.

In the event eleven museums[2] sent representatives, providing a total of fifteen delegates to the meeting. Such an apparently small turnout should be seen first in the context of the strong natural history bias among the prime movers of the Association and the fact that most of those invited were society or private museums, often with honorary curators and little or no money for operational needs. In fact most museums with an annual revenue budget of £400 or more were present; the most obvious absentees were Birmingham (which took no interest in the Association for some years), Ipswich and Leicester. Although the rate-supported museums predominated, two societies were present with five representatives between them.

The delegates received a letter from Professor W H Flower, President-elect of the British Association for the Advancement of Science, expressing his conviction that a museums association was much needed and hoped that it would not be restricted to provincial museums. The meeting duly brought the Museums Association into being and agreed that it should consist of curators, those engaged in active museum work and representatives of the management committees of such museums, although this was varied slightly at the first annual meeting. The subscription was determined at not less than one guinea annually for museums and at a half-guinea a year for associates. When it came to the management of the Association, it was agreed that this should be vested in a President, two secretaries and five other persons each subject to re-election annually; it was further agreed that the President should desirably be chosen from the town at which the next annual meeting would be held.

Having determined that the next meeting of the Association would be in Liverpool, the Revd Henry Higgins (1814–1893) was elected President. Higgins was present in his capacity as Chairman of the Museums Sub-Committee at Liverpool. He had, however, held the Presidency of both the Liverpool Naturalist's Field Club and the Literary and Philosophical Society of Liverpool and had spent over thirty years working voluntarily for the Museum. He appears to have been considered as the Honorary Director of the Museum (Morton, 1894). Certainly, he wrote a number of the Museum's guides and was responsible for the arrangement of a very fine series of the Museum's invertebrates. He also initiated the Museum's school loan scheme. Clearly he worked very closely with Thomas Moore (1824–1892), the Curator of the Liverpool Museum who was elected by the meeting as one of the secretaries of the Association. The other Secretary was Henry Platnauer (1857–1939), Keeper of the Yorkshire Philosophical Society's Museum who commenced his career at the British Museum (Natural History) (Pyrah, 1988). On the face of it the new Association does not appear as the creation of a young and aspiring generation: the President was 75 and one of the secretaries 65 however, this belies the fact that the two main originators of the idea, Howarth and Paton, were aged 24 and 34 respectively when they first wrote to *Nature* twelve years ago. The Committee comprised R Cameron, Honorary Curator of the Sunderland Museum; E Howarth, Curator of the Museum and Art Gallery at Sheffield and the main originator of the Association; B Lomax, Curator of the Brighton Museum; S W North, Vice-President of the Yorkshire Philosophical Society who chaired the initial meetings; and Lieut Col the Alderman H Turner, Chairman of the Stockport Museum Committee.

Having completed the business aspects of the matter, attention then turned to some of the subjects which might be considered by the Association:

1. Means of interchange of duplicate and surplus specimens;
2. Means of securing models, casts and reproductions;
3. Scheme for a general supply of labels, illustrations and information;
4. Uniform plan of arranging Natural History collections;
5. Scheme for securing the services of specialists;
6. Improvement of Libraries and Museums legislation;

7. The indexing of the general contents of museums;
8. The promotion of museum lectures to working men;
9. Preparation of small educational loan collections for circulation among schools;
10. Concerted action for securing Government publications and also specimens, on loan or otherwise;
11. The issue of a Journal by the Association and the collecting of scattered original papers for publication in the said Journal if found possible.

There is no evidence that the Committee elected at York met again until April of the following year and then it was to deal with arrangements for the next annual meeting and other administrative matters. Some of the members travelled to Liverpool for this and three of them met again a month later in Sheffield to complete their business. The programme for the conference was agreed and one of the rules proposed was amended to enable member museums to send three voting representatives to the annual meeting. The circular giving details of the Liverpool conference was sent to all museums in the United Kingdom. The professional issues discussed at the inaugural meeting do not appear to have been considered by the committee at this stage.

Early membership

Early in the history of the Association, associate membership was modified to include persons interested in museums. Although beneficial to the Association fiscally, in that a larger group could attend and participate in the annual conference, this category of membership fluctuated considerably making it difficult to assess the more permanent membership growth. However, by 1899 the Editor of the *Proceedings* indicated that those members directly connected with museums numbered about 64. On this basis comparison with the membership list of 1890 suggests that there were 33 members associated with museums and therefore a virtual doubling of the core membership in the first ten years can be assumed. Certainly most of the major provincial museums are in membership by the end of the century and in the case of Leicester and Ipswich, for example, the curators Montagu Brown and Frank Woolnough respectively held associate membership at least for part of this period.

Although the Association had been established primarily for the benefit of the provincial museums of the United Kingdom at least three of its founding associate members were from nationally funded museums: Professor W H Flower and F A Bather from the British Museum (Natural History) and F W Rudler of the Museum of Practical Geology; the latter and Dr R T Scharff of the National Museum in Dublin were members of the first Council. However, as the decade continued, the lack of other national staff attending the conference resulted in the Council formally writing to the Trustees of the British Museum and to the Science and Art Department, enquiring whether staff would be allowed to attend. Both replied in the affirmative. By 1891 two overseas museums were in full membership, Colombo and Otago, and there was an associate member from Dresden, Dr A B Meyer. It was not until the Oxford meeting in 1897 that the Association's rules were amended to regularize the admission of overseas museums as members by which time Baroda, Cape Town, the Institute of Jamaica, Perth, Salt Lake City and Sydney were already listed as members and the representative of the Deseret Museum from Salt Lake City had been elected a member of the Council.

Another factor influencing membership and also the work of the Association in its early days was its strong natural history bias. This is very apparent in the papers to the 1890 and 1891 conferences. The problem was recognized within the Association and the Editor noted in the 1892 *Proceedings* that the Manchester meeting marked the introduction of papers on art museums and that the work was in no sense limited to science museums. Indeed there was also a plea in one of the conference papers for greater attention to be given by museums to historical material (Hicks, 1892). At the business meeting that year, one of the vice-presidencies was left vacant so that it might be filled by the Director of an art gallery or museum. In the end the first president of the Association with an art background was James Paton of Glasgow, one of the protagonists for the formation of an association fifteen years previously. He took office in 1896.

Early conferences

On Tuesday 17 June 1890 delegates assembled in Liverpool for the first full annual conference of the Association. That evening they heard the President's address in the Brown Lecture Hall of the Museum and afterwards were entertained at a reception and soirée given by the Library, Museum and Arts Committee of the Town Council. Twenty-eight representatives from member museums attended together with some fifty associates who were mostly from the Liverpool area. For the next two days delegates received papers on museum matters in the morning, closing with a short business session, and visited places of interest in the afternoon. Visits were also arranged for the Friday and final day of the conference.

The papers covered such subjects as museum organization and arrangement, the determination of natural history specimens in museums, a new method of mounting invertebrates, museum cases, museum visitors and the best means of making museums attractive to the public. In addition the local team from Liverpool described their Museum and aspects of their work, including the circulating school cabinets and the winter evening lectures. With the adoption of the rules, a Treasurer and Council were elected. The members of the existing committee were elected to the Council together with four additional persons[3], among them three who had written supporting the idea of a museums association in the periodical *Nature* over a decade ago. The conference was ajudged an entire success.

The location of the early conferences were clearly selected with a view to extending the Association's influence to different parts of the United Kingdom: Cambridge, Manchester, London, Dublin, Newcastle, Glasgow and Oxford. The south-east was included with a conference at Brighton in 1899; however, the south-west had to await the meeting in Bristol in 1906 and Wales did not provide a venue until 1914 when the Association met in Swansea; although Cardiff had been a member since 1890, it had declined an invitation to hold it in 1902. Attendance at these conferences involved about thirty representatives of the member museums each year, plus a varying number of associate members who joined in order to attend the conference. Thus in numerical terms the most successful of the early conferences was that at Dublin in 1894 which attracted about 100 delegates; at least two-thirds of these were temporary local members.

Already some of the broad patterns of the way the Association was to conduct its business are emerging. In 1895 the idea of holding popular lectures in association with the conference, based on the British Association model, was proposed but left to the individual hosts to organize if they wished. A proposal to hold the conference every three years in 1897 did not receive support. Sometimes a trade and delegate exhibition would be organized at the conference venue. In financial terms the Association's early years were successful and the Council maintained an increasing surplus which by 1900 had reached nearly £88 (about £30 in excess of the total annual subscription income). Notwithstanding this, the projected monthly publication required considerable outlay and museums were invited to increase their subscriptions; a number did so.

The *Proceedings*

The means of making known museum needs, providing a channel for exchanges and disseminating new ideas about museum arrangement etc. was a matter of some discussion at the first meeting, at which the publication of a journal figured strongly. The Council decided, however, that they could only afford to publish the proceedings of the Liverpool meeting at present. Three members of the Council met during the British Association meeting in September 1890 at Leeds where it was agreed that advertisements should be included in the publication and that the price of this annual publication would be five shillings. Elijah Howarth and Henry Platnauer were appointed as editors. Although a monthly news leaflet had been suggested by Richard Quick of the Horniman Museum in 1898 the Council preferred to work to a more substantial monthly publication. The following year the Library Supply Co of London offered to publish a *Museum Record* under their control for the Association, but the *Proceedings* of the annual meeting remained the main publication until 1901 when the Association had amassed sufficient capital to launch the *Museums Journal*.

The *Proceedings* provided an important medium for communication which, as the publication developed, covered a number of important professional topics, often from a practical standpoint. Of the many papers published, that on the principles of museum administration, read at the Newcastle conference for G Brown Goode (1895), Assistant Secretary of the US National Museum, was regarded as an important statement on the subject for many years and appeared in Museums Association Diploma bibliographies as late as 1957. Another important paper for the time was the description of the installation of electric light in the Manchester Museum (Hoyle, 1898) which, although by no means the first museum to do so, provided a practical insight into the problems and benefits of museum lighting.

Professional debate

A number of issues to which the Association would in due course contribute considerable attention were discussed in these early days. Museum cataloguing, for example, was the subject of papers by Hoyle (1891), Hoyle and Bolton (1894) and, indirectly, Goode (1895); museum legislation received the attention of Howarth (1891) following the introduction of the new *Museums and Gymnasiums Act 1891*. This led to closer collaboration with the Library Association on legislative matters. Also at the annual business meeting of 1891 the members approved the circularization of the new County Councils recommending assistance to museums under the technical education provisions of the *Customs and Excise Act 1890*. They rejected a suggestion, however, that parliament should be petitioned for the teaching of natural history to be made compulsory in all elementary schools.

The provision of specialist aid for museums has also been a recurrent theme through the years. A committee to look into this question was appointed at the Liverpool meeting and the following year suggested that an advisory committee of specialists should be established. The curator of a museum wishing to have a collection named would approach the committee who would advise on an appropriate specialist; thereafter it was a matter between the curator and the specialist. This facility does not seem to have been much used.

The 1893 General Meeting heard from Frederick James, the Curator of the Maidstone Museum, about a scheme proposed by the Kent Archaeological Society to certain of the Boroughs in the county. This involved the appointment of an Inspector of ancient monuments and museums, amongst whose duties would be determining which museums should house archaeological material. Although the scheme had been withdrawn, members condemned the principle on which it was based. Another matter of concern

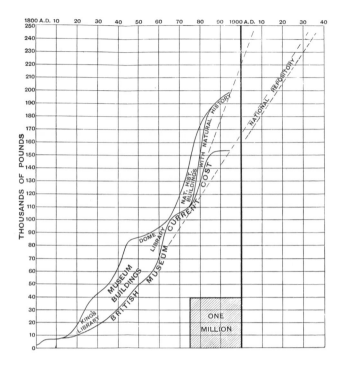

FIG. 3: This graph supported Professor Petrie's argument that the proposed national repository for science and art could be maintained in perpetuity from funds transferred from the British Museum.

to the Association was the lack of information about museums. This was emphasized by Bolton (1898) in a paper to the annual conference which led to the establishment of a committee to look at ways and means of improving this. This led initially to the preparation of a directory of museums which, for cost reasons, was circulated in parts with the *Museums Journal*. Other suggestions discussed included the need for a series of handbooks and an annual bibliography of references to museums and museum work contained in the periodical literature.

Professor W M Flinders Petrie (1897a,b; 1900) contributed many ideas about the operation of museums, often reflecting his concern about the economics of museums. The first suggested a federal staff for museums whereby a group of peripatetic specialists provided assistance to the non-national museums as required. Another suggestion was that the Museums Association should create a trust for collections with the idea that anyone could leave their collections to the trust in the knowledge that the material would be cared for; his scheme included the movement of such collections from one museum to another every twenty or thirty years. A further idea involved a national repository for science and art located about an hour's travelling time from London. This 'store museum', as he called it, could be financed by the 'mere arrest of the growth of the British Museum during five years (Fig 3) with the weeding out of collections and library during that period into the store museum'. This 'would suffice to pay for the whole of it for ever'. His schemes were discussed at meetings of the British Association for the Advancement of Science and the Royal Society of Arts.

Museum labelling

Discussion on labelling, which had been a major criticism of provincial museums, was the subject of a number of papers to the Association's conference. A Committee on Labelling in Museums[4] was established at the Liverpool meeting, and in response to a circular, received sample labels from some seventeen museums and also the views of members on the subject. They reported to the Cambridge and Manchester meetings. It was found that no museum had a regular system of labelling throughout except for the Manchester Museum at Owen's College but name labels without any descriptive text were being used there. With the exception of Manchester, coloured lettering was not in use to any extent and the normal style was black lettering on a white or neutral ground. A number of museums, however, were adopting white lettering on a black or dark ground. Different type sizes were being used to indicate the different levels in the zoological or palaeontological classifications.

The Committee found that the Saffron Walden Museum had some time ago printed a set of labels for British birds and had tried to interest other museums to take copies and so maintain a uniform system of labelling. It was also noted that the small charts showing geological and zoological distributions from Saffron Walden and Nottingham respectively could be adopted in all museums. It was therefore decided to produce some sample labels (Fig 4) to seek comment from members and if favourable for the Association to print sets for sale. It was suggested that if 50 museums subscribed, a complete set of descriptive labels embracing all the principal divisions of the animal kingdom could be made available for thirty-five shillings.

Availability of government reports

At the General Meeting in 1894 it was agreed that a circular be prepared and issued seeking the signatures of member museums who wished to receive the publications of the Geological Survey together with maps and sections for the district in which they were situated. At a Council meeting in July of

SPECIMEN LABEL.

ORDER : RODENTIA.
RODENTS.

The Rodents are more numerous in species than any other order of mammals, are all herbivorous and have a wide distribution, being found in nearly all parts of the world. They all present a great similarity in general structure, and none of them attain a large size, the largest of them being the Capybara. The order is well defined, and at once recognised by the dentition, which consists of 2 prominent incisors in each jaw, premolars and molars, but there are no canines. The Picas, Hares and Rabbits have two pairs of incisors in the upper jaw, the second pair very small. The incisor teeth grow from a permanent pulp, their edges being constantly worn away by gnawing, this gnawing (from which the animals take their name of Rodents or Gnawing Animals) is absolutely necessary to the existence of the animal, for as the teeth are continually growing and take the form of a segment of a circle they would curve round into the mouth if they were not continually worn away, and this actually occurs when a tooth is accidentally fractured. Rodents are very diverse in their habits, some live on trees as, Squirrels ; some have the skin developed into parachutes on their sides and can take flying leaps from tree to tree ; others are runners, such as Hares and Rabbits ; the Jerboas have the hind legs longer than the fore legs and are agile jumpers ; the Mole-rats are diggers ; and the Beavers and Water Voles are aquatic. The fur of many Rodents has a high commercial value such as the Beaver, Squirrel, Chinchilla, &c. The order Rodentia comprises 3 extinct and 18 recent families. The recent families include the following :—(1) Anomalurus ; (2) Squirrels and Marmots ; (3) Haplodon ; (4) Beavers ; (5) Dormice ; (6) Lophiomys ; (7) Rats, Mice and Voles ; (8) Mole-rats ; (9) Pouched Rats ; (10) Jerboas ; (11) Spiny Mice ; (12) Porcupines ; (13) Chinchillas ; (14) Dinomys ; (15) Cavies ; (16) Agouties ; (17) Picas ; (18) Hares and Rabbits.

FIG. 4: This sample label accompanied the Labelling Committee's first report.

the following year, it was decided to send this and the list of signatures to the Director General of the Geological Survey. In July 1886 Council was investigating the cost of supplying member museums with relevant maps and publications from the Geological Survey but thereafter nothing more is heard of either matter.

About the same time member museums were similarly circulated regarding the 'Challenger' reports. Some fifty volumes on this oceanographic exploration were issued between 1880 and 1895 and the Association asked the Stationery Office to send copies to those museums that had signed the circular. Evidently this approach was unsuccessful because the Council subsequently asked Mr R Cameron, MP, who represented the Sunderland Museum and was a member of the Association's Council, to put a question in the House of Commons as to which museums the 'Challenger' reports were being distributed. In 1899 museums were advised in the *Proceedings* to apply to the Royal Society if they wished to receive copies of the report. The remaining duplicate specimens from the expedition were offered to public museums by the British Museum (Natural History).

Science and Art Department services

In 1896 a Committee of the House of Commons was set up to look at the museums of the Department of Science and Art. An issue of particular concern to provincial museums was the Circulation Department which had provided loans of objects for some years. Because there had been some criticism of the Department in the press, the Association passed a resolution at its Oxford meeting recording the importance and value of the circulation system to provincial museums and also sought that the scheme might be greatly extended. The ensuing report of the Committee recommended an increase in the collections to be available under the scheme.

Another of the services to provincial museums was the grant-in-aid for museum purchases which had been instituted in 1881. At that time £1500 had been voted for the purpose each year, but now due to the lack of demand and a Departmental rule that preference would be given to supporting the purchase of reproductions, the annual figure stood at £500. At the 1898 conference the Association sought an increase of the annual grant to £3000; in the event an additional £250 was allocated for 1899.

CHAPTER THREE

INTO THE TWENTIETH CENTURY

A decade had passed since the Association's inauguration. It had doubled its membership in that time and developed into an established national organization, recognized internationally, with increased responsibilities and membership expectations. It was no longer reasonable to expect the whole elected Council, which met only two or three times during the period of the annual conference each year, to continue as the policy determining and executive body. Re-assessment was necessary. Accordingly the Council determined that an Executive Committee should be formed and this was endorsed by the Business Meeting on 6 July 1899. The Committee met six weeks later at Sheffield, appointing the Treasurer, Alderman W H Brittain as their Chairman, and then on two further occasions before the next annual conference.

The *Museums Journal*

The Association's publications took a fair amount of the new Executive Committee's time at its first meetings. There had been an overspending on the 1898 *Proceedings*, which had to be resolved. The detailed work for the new monthly publication to be launched in 1901 also fell on the Committee. This was known as *Musea* until very late in the planning stage when the title *Museums Journal* was decided. In recognition of the foreign membership, it established a small overseas editorial group to assist the Editor. The transition from the annual *Proceedings* to a monthly *Journal* inevitably had a marked effect on the Association's workload and, for that matter, on the nature of the publication. As well as being the organ for publishing the proceedings of its annual meetings it was now intended to provide current news of museums and art galleries, reports on museums, descriptive illustrated articles, notes and queries, correspondence, book reviews and provide a medium for making known offers of exchange and sale. The need to maintain a good balance between these and to ensure the continuing publication of articles of substance was a matter of concern to the Executive Committee. This seems to have been the reason why a

FIG. 5: Weston Park Museum, Sheffield, *c* 1900, where the Association's Executive Committee often met. The first Chairman and Secretary of the Committee were from Sheffield.

specific conference theme was selected for 1905 – the relationship between provincial and national museums – so that the next issue of the *Journal* could be devoted to the subject.

The proposal was successful in that it exposed a number of different viewpoints about the role of the State in both national and provincial museum provision. There were those who argued that the government should take on a real responsibility for the major museums in the provinces, providing grant on a similar basis to that applying to the University Colleges' Grant with the county councils subsidizing the remaining museums provided they met the requirements of an annual inspection (Bolton 1906). Then there were those who believed that museums tended to be more successful if they were independent of Government. With regard to the national museum collections the case was argued for the present loan arrangements from the Victoria and Albert Museum to be extended to include the British Museum (Minto 1906) while another speaker called for all important items to go to the national collection (Mosley 1906). These issues foreshadowed a number of debates that would take place within the Association in the coming years.

The reader of early volumes of the *Journal* will be struck by the number of papers by overseas contributors and the emphasis on practical aspects of museum work. At a very fundamental level there are such articles

FIG 6: Alderman W H Brittain of Sheffield, the Association's first Treasurer and Chairman of its Executive Committee. He was President in 1898.

as 'Business devices for the curator', written by a Fellow of the Royal Society, who describes in some detail basic office equipment such as the typewriter, etc. (Bather 1910). This is a reminder of the breadth of duties that fell on the provincial museum curator at this time. More directly related to curatorship are the papers on museum cases and fittings, a number of which were delivered at the Bristol conference; one of them, by Bather (1907), discusses interchangeability in display cases and drawers which is effectively a modular system. Another topic which continued to be regularly treated was the registration and cataloguing of museum collections. At this time Hoyle (1901) was writing on useful applications for card catalogues while Lowe (1903) discussed in some detail the system in use at Plymouth. Wray (1905), who had been in Britain for some months looking at museum practice, returned to the Perek State Museum where he introduced a system which dispensed with registers and relied entirely on two card indexes, one in numerical order and the other classified.

An editorial in the Journal suggested that volunteers, drawn from the learned societies, universities and colleges could greatly assist in the cataloguing of museum collections (Museums Association 1903a). An extension of the volunteer help concept was the Norwich Museum Association which was created to support the Museum in its scientific work and help in providing lectures. In describing its work and the need for lecturing support, Frank Leney (1909) commented 'it seemed at one time as if a lecturer on "Nature Study" would be added to the museum staff. . . Happily for the Museum, I think, it was found that funds would not permit the appointment'.

Museum information

The Executive Committee was also responsible for compiling the question-naire seeking information prior to the publication of a directory of museums. The need for sound information about the museums of Britain was recognized at an early stage in the Association. Indeed it had had the advantage at its inception of the tables of data about provincial museums in Britain prepared by the British Association (1887). But the number of museums were increasing rapidly and information about existing museums was changing considerably. It was for such reasons that the Association decided to issue a directory, the first edition of which was serialized in the *Museums Journal* for about four years from September 1902. Unlike the earlier lists, the information did not follow a set format because of the variety of the information provided. The quality of the statistical and other information available to the Association, however, was the subject of some comment in the first volume of the *Journal*.

Very occasionally information about museum practice would come from an independent source. Dr A B Meyer, the Director of the Dresden Museums, had joined the Museums Association in 1891. In 1902 he was asked by his government to review museum practice in Britain and the United States. Comments from the resulting report were published in the *Journal* by Bather (1903). He paid some attention to museum climatology and was clearly impressed with the Plenum system of air conditioning which he found at the Museum and Art Gallery at Glasgow and the Liverpool Museum. He comments on the fact that both had installed the system independently and that neither knew that the other was using it. On the effect of light on collections he was far more critical and had this to say in the context of the British Museum (Natural History):

> It is the rule in England to open collections to the public during the whole of the day and the museum people say they cannot manage otherwise or they would have no money voted to them. But I think they are making a mistake. If only the officials themselves were thoroughly impressed with the damage suffered by the collections ... they would readily convince the authorities.

Meyer also expresses his disappointment at the ethnological collections at the British Museum. 'Considering the world domination of Great Britain,' he writes, 'it ought to have been the natural task of the British Museum to take the lead in ethnography; whereas the collection is scarcely greater than that of several continental collections and is left far behind by the magnificent collection at Berlin.'

Another matter discussed by the Executive Committee was the Association's unincorporated status. This arose initially because of the Committee's wish to invest some of its surplus funds, but became more poignant when one of the advertisers in the Journal became bankrupt and the Association was barred from proving its case because it was unincorporated. After a number of enquiries over some years about the registration of the Association and limited liability company status, it eventually decided just to appoint two trustees to manage the Association's investments, the costs of realising corporate status being considered too high. The increased work of the Association was also reflected in the decision to appoint an assistant secretary. However, the pressures of the time did not prevent the Secretary from sending a letter of congratulation and best wishes for the success of the newly formed American Association of Museums in 1906. Another association for curators on similar lines was founded in Sweden in the same year. There was now also the *Verband der Museumsdirektoren* which had been founded in 1897 by Professor Brinckmann of Hamburg and Dr Angst of Zurich to try to counteract the problem of fakes, forgeries and fraud. This Germanic group, however, widened its brief to include other technical matters and by 1902 involved eighty-four heads of European museums and had held its annual meetings in London and Copenhagen (Koetschau 1902; Meyer 1903).

Annual conference

The planning of the annual conference also fell to the lot of the Executive Committee. In 1902, continuing its wish to cater for the overseas membership, it contacted Dr Brünchorst of the Bergens Museum, Bergen with a view to holding the 1904 conference in Norway. This, however, was not possible and the Association had to wait another sixteen years for its first overseas conference. Despite this, when the Council came to write their annual report in 1904, they were in self-congratulatory mood. They reviewed the increasing membership, the larger *Journal* and the usefulness of the Directory published in it, the successful conferences which were attracting overseas delegates, and a satisfactory financial situation. In conclusion they felt that they could 'sincerely congratulate the Association on its advancing prosperity, greater activity and expanding usefulness'. Indeed the annual meeting was so popular that no less than six invitations were received to host it in 1907.

It should be noted that the Association's annual meeting was not the only means of contact for curators. A Saturday conference was held in Warrington in October 1904 and attracted over thirty delegates; others were held at about six-month intervals in Bolton, Keighley, Chester and Salford. The first of these north-west England museums conferences had been held at Manchester where Charles Madeley (1904) had advocated the idea of a county museum service. He pointed out that in a rural district the formation and maintenance of an efficient museum was scarcely practicable. But, just as the provision of education services had become a county function to overcome the same problem, so museums should be similarly treated. Under his proposal district museums would be established and managed by a county director of museums who would advise and consult with a local committee formed for each of the museums. He saw such museums having an overtly educational function but also satisfying and cultivating the taste of the adult visitor.

Educational work

A very strong sense of educational purpose pervades a number of the articles in the *Journal* and the papers to the conferences, sometimes apparently to the exclusion of any consideration that museums might also be enjoyable. This was certainly not the case with Frank Woolnough (1904) who described the Ipswich Museum's work in nature study at the Norwich conference. Woolnough was a well-known character in the Association's early days who enlivened many an annual dinner with his wit and who, incidentally, wrote the letter announcing his own death to the Editor of the *Journal*. In another contribution to that conference, Henry Coates and Alex Rodger (1905) brought members up-to-date on a successful natural history competition organized by the Perthshire Natural History Museum and which they had first reported at the 1899 conference. The papers generated a lively discussion and this, together with a list of nature study facilities offered by museums and gardens in and near London published in the *Journal*, gives an indication of the extent of nature study work in museums.

The recognition of instruction in a museum as school attendance in the Day School Code of 1894 had meant a closer association between educationists and curators, although the requirement that the number of children should not exceed fifteen in order to qualify under the Code was a restriction. In 1902 the Director of the Manchester Museum was invited to read a paper at the North of England Educational Conference and spoke on the use of museums in teaching (Hoyle 1903). He particularly argued that curatorial staff should teach the teachers how to use the museum rather than endeavouring to teach the children direct, and spoke of the lack of support from public elementary school teachers in his attempts to organize classes for teachers. On another occasion the President and the Secretary represented the Association at the Federal Conference on Education held in London in 1907. One section of the conference dealt with Museums and Education to which Dr Frederic Kenyon of the British Museum read a paper; the conference unanimously resolved that there should be closer union between museums and schools.

Lord Sudeley's work

The campaign of Lord Sudeley (1840–1922) for greater recognition of the public utility of museums commenced in 1910 (Sudeley 1911). This found particular expression in promoting the appointment of guide lecturers in museums, on which subject he wrote to *The Times* in October of that year. His campaign met with some success in the national museums and indeed he was responsible for introducing a debate on the subject in the House of Lords in April 1913. The Museums Association (1903b) had not always wholeheartedly supported the idea of museum lectures and in one *Journal* editorial it was stated that 'a lecture may be a good thing and a museum may be a good thing, but a museum-lecture is exeedingly unsatisfactory'. However, the use of guide lecturers was appreciatively discussed at its Hull conference (Hallett 1913; Leonard 1914). Lord Sudeley attempted to extend the idea to local museums and applied to the Carnegie United Kingdom Trust for £2,500 over five years to achieve this (Sudeley 1915). However, his application was unsuccessful but some provincial museums did introduce guide lecturers. He joined the Association in 1912 and clearly supported many of its ideals, corresponding with the officers of the Association on a number of issues. Lord Sudeley was made an honorary member of the Association in 1917 but declined the presidency a few years later.

National developments

The Association continued to watch national developments by government and others in London and elsewhere. In 1908 the British Museum (Natural History) advertized the post of Keeper of the Zoological Department which, a correspondent to The Times announced, had never taken place before. If a zoologist not on the Museum staff is appointed, he commented, 'the trustees can hardly expect any of the younger and promising assistants to stay' (Webb 1908). The following year another letter was written to *The Times*, this time criticizing the administration of the Museum at Trustee level and particularly for the fact that the Director was responsible to the Librarian at Bloomsbury (Ewart *et al* 1909). At the Brighton conference in 1911 a resolution was passed expressing concern that the site allocated by the Bell Committee for the Science Museum in South Kensington would encroach on land previously earmarked for the British Museum (Natural History).

About this time other European countries were following the Scandinavian lead in developing national folk museums and the issue was taken up for Britain by Henry Balfour (1912), first as President of the Association. A proposal to establish an open air museum of British folk-life in the grounds of Crystal Palace, presented at the 1913 business meeting of the Association, drew cordial support and encouragement to the Lord Mayor of London to carry the suggestion into effect. The Association's Council also noted the growth of the National Trust, founded in 1895 but considerably strengthened by legislation passed in 1907. It looked at ways of collaboration with the Trust and in 1914 sought to nominate a representative on its Council, which was declined.

The review of the grant-in-aid procedure to assist purchases for provincial museums by a Departmental Committee in 1910 provided an opportunity for the Association to press the case for grant-aiding scientific material. A request for the Board of Education to make a statement at the Association's conference, however, was declined on the grounds that the study should be completed first. As no progress had been achieved by 1913 a deputation was arranged by the Museums Association to meet members of the Science Museum's Advisory Council who asked for a follow-up report as to the directions in which the grant might be given and the conditions that should be applied. This was prepared and could be interpreted as seeking an extension of the scheme to cover all other types of museum object. However, after consideration by the Advisory Council it was duly passed to the Board of Education and at the 1914 conference the Honorary Secretary was able to report that the scheme had been extended to scientific material. Indeed it was used during the war years to aid the purchase of small cases illustrating various pests, among others those injurious to allotments, market gardens and forest trees.

The loan of objects from the national museums and galleries to the provincial institutions has been debated throughout the existence of the Association. J Charlton Deas (1911) raised the issue of national art loans in the *Journal* and Council examined the matter. This was the subject of a resolution at the Brighton conference where it was pointed out that there were already 233 pictures from the National Gallery on loan to provincial museums and galleries. Sympathy for the proposal was expressed although there could be no immediate action while the extensions to the National Gallery were in progress. In 1913 the Victoria and Albert Museum's Circulation Department became a self-contained unit with its own collections for loan to provincial museums. With the expansion of the local museums and therefore the demands on the service, the Association in conference that year sought a considerable augmentation of the Department's collection so that it could better meet the demands made on it. As the situation did not improve, the Association asked the President of the Board of Education to receive a deputation on the matter in 1914. However, the following year the Victoria and Albert Museum sought the views of the Association regarding the temporary suspension of the loans scheme to which the Association reluctantly agreed. In November 1918, however, the Executive Committee asked the Secretary of the Board of Education to reinstate the service as a matter of urgency in the interests of industrial art education.

The question of the liability of museums, art galleries and libraries to pay rates has been a recurrent theme for much of the life of the Association. In 1905 a ruling went against the Corporation of Liverpool in its attempt to maintain exemption for its library under the *Scientific Societies Act 1843* and this was reported in the *Journal* (Museums Association 1905). At the Dublin conference T V Hodgson of Plymouth raised the question of the liability or otherwise of museums and galleries to pay rates and the Association's Executive Committee was asked to examine the matter. It subsequently learned that the problems which had given rise to the difficulties at Plymouth, and at Birmingham, had been resolved. Counsel's opinion however was sought, particularly in relation to the exemptions granted under the 1843 Act. A survey of current practice also took place and a subsequent conference was told that forty-six replies had been received although 'the information did not lend itself to summary'. The issue arose again in the 1950s when the Rating Committee of the Museums Association (1954) made a useful statement on the matter.

CHAPTER FOUR

THE GREAT WAR AND ITS AFTERMATH

T he Association had an excellent conference in Swansea in July 1914 and particular mention was made in the vote of thanks to their hosts of the lavish hospitality and splendid organization that had been provided. The Council had reported a satisfactory conclusion to two of its enquiries, and the annual meeting had agreed to an amendment of the rules so that the President would in future be elected by the Council. Council was also asked to try to arrange the next conference in Paris. As Taylor (1965) has said of this time 'a sensible, law-abiding Englishman could pass through life and hardly notice the existence of the state'. This is unlikely to be the reason for the apparent total unawareness of the gathering cloud over Europe; more likely, it was the spirit of neutralism which was widespread in Britain at the time and perhaps also a feeling of comradeship for continental colleagues under threat. Within a month, the Kaiser's armies were advancing through Belgium towards Paris. The idea of a continental conference was dead even before the August issue of the *Journal* announcing it had reached the members. Thereafter the question was whether there would be a shortened conference, without hospitality or excursion, in London. The decision to proceed was not made until March 1915.

The affect of the War on the Association was considerable. Until 1918 the rule requiring the election of Council was suspended and, except for the replacement of vacancies, the same officers and members remained in power. It also affected the form of the annual meetings which were much reduced in length and in 1917 comprised only one day in July at the Victoria and Albert Museum to conduct a business meeting. Twenty-four people attended this, fifteen of whom were members of the Council anyway. At that meeting a difference of opinion arose regarding the need for discussion on a number of urgent national matters; the meeting adjourned on the basis that a further meeting would be arranged in October if there was sufficient support. The support did not materialize but Elijah Howarth decided, independently, to call a conference on the relation of museums to education and local war museums. The exact circumstances which led to this conference are unclear, and although the preface of the report (Howarth 1918) refers to 'a conference of members of the Museums Association and representatives of all provincial museums', the Association's attitude to the meeting is ambivalent[5]. It is also unclear why Howarth, despite apparent agreement with the idea of returning to an annually elected Council at the 1917 business meeting, should seek the following year to establish a Provisional (Wartime) Committee for the duration of the War, a proposal which was ruled out of order by the Council.

The story of the Association's role in the aborted idea of local war museums, about which the 1917 conference and the Sheffield meeting were much concerned, has been told elsewhere (Kavanagh 1984). Another concern of members, of a very different nature, figured in the Association's minutes and *Journal* for a considerable time; this was the supply of rectangular glass specimen jars used to house spirit collections. These jars, which had been imported from Germany, were no longer available and the optical quality of cylindrical jars was inferior when viewing the specimens. The Honorary Secretary reported back on a possible solution in a letter to the *Journal* in April 1916 and during the business meeting of that year but the supply of specimen jars remained an issue well after the war was over. The *Journal* itself was another increasing burden as printing and paper costs increased. In 1916 this monthly publication was reduced from 32 to 24 pages and for a period suffered further reduction. Then there was the question of the German members, five museums and seven associates, whose subscriptions remained unpaid. Council decided in 1916 to take no action and there the matter rested until the annual business meeting two years later when the the rules relating to the lapsed members were applied.

The Birmingham Museum and Art Gallery was admitted into membership of the Association in May 1916; neither the Museum nor its staff had joined in the early days although W H Edwards, who is credited with having created the best natural history displays in the provinces (Davies 1985), had become an associate member in 1912. About this time, the tax assessor at Birmingham had levied income tax on the presumed annual rental value of those parts of the building used for art purposes. The Museum had won an appeal against this but the matter was likely to go to the High Court. The Association's Council, therefore, was greatly concerned at the impact this would have generally if the case went against Birmingham and, apart from encouraging the local authority to resist the proposal strenuously, made a donation of £10 towards the expenses involved to mark the sense of the importance of the issue. The action had the unanimous support of the annual business meeting which decided to enlist the help of the Board of Education and also encouraged members to inform their members of parliament. The following year it was reported that a temporary and confidential compromise had been reached by Birmingham with the income tax authorities at which Council expressed its regret.

In January 1916, the Executive Committee learned that Newport Museum was considering closure for economic reasons and they accordingly wrote pointing out that they were unique in this retrograde step in the provinces. But earlier in the month the National Portrait Gallery had closed and the Wallace Collection had followed. The Government's Committee on Retrenchment (1916) issued a White Paper on 1 February recommending that, with the possible exception of the Reading Room at the British Museum, all museums should close. The national museums cost about £300,000 a year and generated income of only about £3,000; their closure would be a valuable object lesson in economy, the Committee stated, and the buildings could be redeployed. On 10 February the Prime Minister received a deputation from the National Art-Collections Fund, the Museums Association (1916) and the Imperial Arts League. The Association brought with it a petition opposing the closure of museums containing 800 names gathered in two days; this included the signatures of six Lords Mayor or Provost, the Mayors of ten provincial towns, ninety academics in fifteen different universities including the Vice-Chancellors of four of them, as well as the names of many others eminent in the field of art, science and education. The Prime Minister was told that about twelve million visitors a year came to provincial museums, and as far as it was possible to assess there had been no decline in the number of home visits because of the war, as was being alleged; a significant number of visits by soldiers and other uniformed visitors were being observed. The museum had an important and topical educational role to play and even if a museum closed there were still continuing costs to maintain the collection and the Government had not taken this into account. When the Government implemented their plan, the Association could legitimately take some credit for the fact that the popular parts of the British Museum (Natural History) remained open and that there would be no requirement for local authorities to close their museums.

Two years later, the War Cabinet announced that it was taking over the British Museum at Bloomsbury for the Air Ministry and the South Kensington premises for other departmental purposes. The Museums Association had already protested at the requisitioning of parts of the Victoria and Albert Museum to provide offices for the Board of Education. Now the nation's greatest museum was being placed at considerable risk by being required to house a department involved in war operations. The Association again wrote to the Premier deploring the position and seeking to send a deputation; the membership was also apprised of the danger by circular letter so that they could react. The Government, however, withdrew their proposals and a few days later the Association received a letter from the Trustees of the British Museum thanking them for their part in the action.

Towards the end of the war, the Secretary of the Association was seconded to the Ministry of Food and in February 1918 every museum received a letter from him in this capacity advocating the preparation of exhibitions to promote food economy. A number of museums had been organizing exhibitions in support of the war effort already. Indeed, the Association had encouraged this from the outset and in the initial euphoria Bather (1915) had exorted members 'to throw away the black coat of respectability and don the blue overalls or the serviceable khaki!' Now, with an acute food shortage the injunction had a certain reality and urgency about it.

Perspectives began to lengthen as the war drew to a close. By July 1918 there was an item on the Council agenda concerning the post-war administration of the Association and the business meeting passed a resolution seeking to give the Association and its work greater publicity. But there were more immediate concerns as well. A resolution was forwarded to the Prime Minister seeking that all objects taken from museums by the Germans should be returned or replaced with an item of equivalent value. The financial difficulties of the museums at home were also the subject of discussion and it was agreed to support the Library Association in seeking the abolition of the rate limit and also to prepare a memorandum for the Adult Education Committee of the Ministry of Reconstruction. Subsequently, the Secretary wrote to the First Commissioner of Works to seek the early release of museums occupied by various Government departments.

Museums in relation to education

In 1913 the British Association for the Advancement of Science formed a Committee on museums in relation to education[6]. This originated from discussion in the Educational Science section that followed papers by Dr Joseph Clubb (1913a) of Liverpool and Mr A R Horwood (1913) of Leicester. The full terms of reference for the Committee were 'to examine, inquire into and report on the character, work and maintenance of museums, with a view to their organization and development as institutions for education and research; and especially to inquire into the requirements of schools'. A grant of £10 was made towards the work. The Committee met regularly until the gravity of the war prevented it with the result that the publication of the Report was delayed (British Association 1920). The Museums Association was closely involved with the work: at the 1915 conference a day was spent on the topic with the Chairman of the Committee; Dr Clubb (1916) presented a further paper at the next annual conference and, if it had taken place, there would have been further discussion at the adjourned meeting of 1917. As it was, the issue was discussed at the Sheffield meeting organized by Elijah Howarth (1918). The Committee also examined the educational work of certain museums in Australia and the United States and their comments on them form an appendix to the report, as does commentary on the schools work introduced at the Manchester Museum by the Education Authority there at the beginning of the war.

The core of the report is based on the 134 responses to a questionnaire sent to the museums of Britain. The conclusions are wide ranging. The Committee took the view that museums can and should develop into centres for research with far better facilities for the advanced student; that a list of the principal contents of all provincial museums should be compiled; that grant-in-aid on a liberal scale should be available if museum educational and research work is to be developed; that the national museums and universities have particular responsibilities for curatorial training and that for schools work special circulating loan collections should be developed.

The British Association was not the only advocate of the educational function of museums at the time. The Ministry of Reconstruction (1919a) reported through its Adult Education Committee that 'the public libraries and museums should be transferred forthwith to the Board of Education'. At the 1919 Conference, Ernest Lowe (1920a) questioned whether it was 'the primary function of a museum or a museum man to serve the purpose of education as we ordinarily understand it'. The view that 'a museum is not fundamentally an educational institution' was subsequently expressed by a correspondent in *Nature* who considered, rather than transferring museums to the Board of Education, that 'provincial museums may be linked up with one another and with the national museums above and the minor museums below, but through a body representative of their own committees and curators' (Anon 1919). The Association's Council established a special committee and the issue was put to representatives of the Board of Education; little hope was gained from this meeting that there had been any real appreciation of the museums' full role in society or of the Association's view that museums should not be transferred to the Board of Education, a view shared, incidentally, by the Library Association in respect of libraries. The Association's members could only await the legislation which would effect these changes.

A new Education Act had passed through Parliament in 1918. This provided a number of reforms to schools and the school leaving age in England and Wales – there was a separate Act for Scotland – and, incidentally, permitted Local Education Authorities to grant-aid a museum and school visits for instructional purposes. When the *Public Libraries Act 1919* reached the statute book there was no compulsory transfer of either libraries or museums to the education authorities, only a clause permitting the voluntary delegation of a library and museum authority's powers to an education authority. Further, the limit on rate-borne expenditure, which had been a restraint to development, was removed and county councils acquired museum powers for the first time. Between them the two Acts met all the objections and most of the issues for which the Association had been striving, as far as English and Welsh museums were concerned. For Ernest

Lowe (1920b), who brought this new information to the Conference the following year, there was cause to rejoice: 'I cannot help feeling the museums and art galleries have now received their charter,' he said.

Staffing and salaries

New issues were now under consideration by the Council. Museums were having difficulty in filling curatorial posts and at the suggestion of the Director of the Victoria and Albert Museum a register of vacancies and of potential applicants was maintained by the Association and the former listed in the *Journal*. One of the reasons for being unable to fill posts was believed to be low salaries and the Council accordingly examined curators' salary scales; it also maintained a watching brief on the current Whitley Council discussions on salaries for local government officials. At a special Council meeting called in October 1920 it was agreed to prepare a salary scale for local government curators, based on the rateable value of the town concerned. Discussions with the Whitley Council and with NALGO eventually led to revisions and in 1922 a recommended salary scale, based on population, was published in the *Journal*.

Financial matters and Geddes' axe

The position of museums regarding local and national taxation recurred under a number of different guises. Were museums eligible for rate relief in view of the scientific and cultural nature of their activities? The Association followed up the Local Rating Bill 1923 in the hope that museums and galleries might receive statutory relief from local rates. As charitable bodies were museums exempt from taxation? It spent some months investigating the case of the West Highland Museum which was being charged entertainment tax, the Association eventually receiving a dispensation on behalf of the Museum, provided assurances were given that no music or other extraneous attractions would be provided. Two years later in 1925, the Association identified with the British Association for the Advancement of Science to seek remission of income tax, which was being charged on a number of learned societies. The difficulty remained for many years.

The increasingly stringent economic circumstances of the early 1920s began to put a brake on the post-war recovery of the museums. The Government's committee on public expenditure, chaired by Sir Eric Geddes, produced a series of reports recommending drastic budgetary cuts early in 1922. These included the abolition of five government departments and major reductions elsewhere; education was particularly badly hit and included reductions in teachers' salaries. The last of the Committee's reports dealt with the trustee national museums. A reduction of £100,000 was expected on the net estimated expenditure of about £506,000 the previous year. The report pointed out that over eighty per cent of expenditure on these museums was on personnel and this was where the major cuts were expected. The Geddes Committee then went on to suggest that revenue might be 'considerably increased' by the imposition of a small entrance fee on certain days of the week and considered that £10,000 might be raised in this way. The Museums Association (1922), which had consistently opposed the principle of admission charges, maintained its stance and directed attention instead to the new Imperial War Museum, albeit in temporary premises. 'Let the objects be stored . . . and in the meantime save the bulk of the £60,000 a year,' the Editor of the *Journal* suggested. For the Board of Education museums there were similar recommendations and cuts, but one issue, which would affect many of the Association's members, was severely criticized. This was the proposal to charge half the actual cost of transporting loan collections to the borrowing museum. This disadvantaged the museums a great distance from London and a return to a uniform lending charge for all was sought.

Indeed the Association was becoming increasingly concerned about the Circulation Department of the Victoria and Albert Museum. By July 1922 the Keepership of the department had already been vacant for eighteen months and the service to provincial museums was deteriorating. The Association had sought representation on the Museum's Advisory Board the previous year but this was declined by the Minister for Education. With the national teachers organizations, the Museums Association had formed a joint committee to establish how far the Circulation Department was meeting the needs of the provinces. The resulting report (Howarth *et al* 1923) reviewed the provision and made recommendations for schools of art, secondary schools and provincial museums. As far as the latter was concerned, the inadequacy of the collection, both in quality and quantity, was clearly stated as well as the grant made available to maintain and supplement it. The President of the Board of Education was asked to extend to the provinces, as far as possible, those art education facilities enjoyed by the metropolis.

One of the original goals of the Association was to improve legislation relating to museums. However, the British Museum Bill No 2, giving power to lend certain types of objects to provincial museums, passed through the House of Commons without consultation or comment in the summer of 1924. The type of material to which the Bill referred was very restrictive and on learning of it the President wrote to the Prime Minister asking that the Association, representing provincial museums, be given the opportunity to explain the needs of local museums and that the Bill be suspended for the meantime. When it became law as the *British Museum Act 1924*, the clauses restricting the type of material available had been modified, much to the relief of the Association. At the same time the Association also expressed its concern to the Prime Minister at the prolonged closure of the Museum of Practical Geology in London.

Member services

In 1922 the Association established a number of committees to consider specific issues, provide information and help members with their enquiries. These covered such subjects as the preservation and restoration of pictures, cements and adhesives and, later, a committee on preservation which was concerned with natural history preparation, fixing and preservation fluids. These committees collected formulae and compiled bibliographies which were available to members on request. The committee whose work was best known, however, resulted from a suggestion by E Rimbault Dibdin (1922) on circulating art exhibitions. Initially a collection of about 100 oil paintings by contemporary British artists was made and organized for circulation to a number of provincial galleries. The success of the scheme resulted in arranging further exhibitions which in due course extended to watercolours, colour prints and sculpture and which continued for some years; one of the exhibitions travelled to South Africa where it had a successful showing at eight galleries before returning to England. From the income resulting from sales and fees from the galleries, the Association took a small commission and extracted the costs of organization.

Colonial and international affairs

The Association's links with overseas museums and particularly those of the British colonies were strong; indeed, incomplete though it was, the first of the separately published directories (Howarth and Platnauer 1911) had included a section on Indian and colonial museums. In 1916 the Executive Committee, following a conference session in which the speaker (Skinner 1916) had sought closer links with the colonies, had written to the principal colonial museums on this, but there had been no follow-up to the proposal. It was, therefore, a perfectly logical decision of the Council, in 1921, to explore the possibility of an exhibition or conference during the forthcoming British Empire Exhibition to take place at Wembley in 1924. Arrangements were made to hold the annual conference there and the exhibition authorities made a hall available for the meetings. The conference included a tour of the exhibition. This does not, however, seem to have been an occasion when the Association developed its policy towards Empire museums. An appeal for greater collaboration with museums in the Dominions did arise following a paper by E C Chubb (1929) of the Durban Museum at the Glasgow conference and the idea of setting up Dominion sections was subsequently agreed by Council. However, the major impetus to the Association's Empire work came with the grant from the Carnegie Corporation of New York in 1931 to undertake surveys in Canada and, later, elsewhere (see chapter 7).

The establishment of an International Museums Office through the International Institute of Intellectual Co-operation and its formal authorization by the League of Nations in July 1926, was discussed by the Association's Executive Committee in April 1927. It does not seem to have been involved in these or the founding discussions. The Committee agreed that the Association should associate with it and seek to have a representative on the governing body. A note in the *Journal* followed but there does not seem to have been a close link with the Office; rather the Office maintained contact direct with the national museums. Sir Cecil Harcourt Smith acted as the Association's delegate at a conference on the examination and preservation of works of art in 1930. This was after the periodical of the International Museums Office, *Mouseion*, had carried a brief history of the Association by Bather (1929) and a report of the Worthing conference.

CHAPTER FIVE

BEATING THE BIG DRUM!

L ord Sudeley had died at the end of 1922. This was a considerable loss to the Association and to the museum movement generally. Two years later a group of his supporters formed themselves into a Sudeley Committee under the chairmanship of Lord Northbourne (1924) to further his work for museums, both in London and the provinces; they continued to promote the idea of public lectures. Other aspects of their work were outlined by Lord Northbourne (1927) in a letter to *The Times* and included lobbying for evening opening at the National Gallery as well as the British Museum where they were anxious to see the installation of a lift to the upper galleries and for the Museum to maintain its Sunday lectures. They also believed that there should be a comprehensive museum and art gallery for the East End of London and were of the opinion that the Bethnal Green Museum should be adapted for this purpose. The Sudeley Committee continued in existence until the beginning of the Second World War.

That Lord Sudeley had believed for some time a Royal Commission on Museums was necessary is revealed in correspondence between him and W E Hoyle (1920). At the Leicester conference, J Bailey (1922) pressed the case and although a number of senior members of the Association called for caution their amendment was lost. A resolution asking for the appointment of a Royal Commission was therefore forwarded to the Prime Minister but it did not receive support because, it was rumoured, the national museum directors would not welcome it. It was unlikely, anyway, that the Government would wish to create a Royal Commission to examine the provincial museums, which were, after all, a local government responsibility.

The matter rested for about two years, though with increasing frustration amongst those concerned with the plight of the provincial museums. The issue erupted again in early 1925, when *The Times* carried two articles about the national museums and the need for their continuous growth, implying further extensions to the British Museum at Bloomsbury. The plight of the provincial museums had been ignored yet again. This led to an editorial in the *Journal* entitled 'Beating the big drum', which was off-printed and circulated to members of parliament through local museum committees together with a statement calling for opposition to any further extensions to the British Museum until the more pressing claims of the provincial museums had been considered. This resulted in questions in parliament and a promise that the President of the Board of Education would investigate the matter.

London vs. prov. museums

In the meantime the Government's priorities were necessarily directed to the country's economic situation and to a General Strike. The Strike does not seem to have interfered with the Association's normal activities; the *Journal* appeared on time and the planned meetings of the Executive Committee did not coincide with the period of major disruption. Association business continued and, apart from routine matters, Council placed on record its congratulations to Elijah Howarth on completing fifty years as Curator of the Sheffield Museum and Art Gallery. They also, at the request of the Association of Municipal Treasurers and Accountants, examined the standard form of accounts for museums and suggested some minor amendments; they also heard that the representations made by the Association regarding the abolition of the post of Curator at the Reading Museum had been successful and that an appointment would now be made. Another ongoing matter concerned the Carnegie United Kingdom Trust and it was reported that their meeting with representatives of educational and local bodies had unanimously supported – as had the Council – the proposal to prepare a report on municipal and other local museums as a factor in education. Was this to be the examination of provincial museums which it had been hoped would be undertaken by a Royal Commission?

It was at this time that Council received the silver-gilt badge and chain[7] which has been worn by generations of Presidents on formal occasions. This was presented to the Association by James Downs of Hull. He attended the Association's conferences for a time as a representative of Hull Museums, which benefited considerably from his support and benefaction, and he was later an associate member of the Association until his death in 1943. The badge, which has had its critics, originally included a clasp and chain with tablets bearing the names of past-presidents. The clasp and chain are no longer used and since 1956 the badge has been worn suspended from a simple blue ribbon.

When the Executive Committee held their autumn meeting in 1926 they considered a letter from Dr Ernest Lowe, a past-president, suggesting that the Association should now consider an office headquarters in London. He suggested that joint tenure of premises with the Library Association might be possible. However, the President proposed that preference should be shown to sharing facilities with a scientific society and it was decided to enquire of the societies in Burlington House first. The Association had had storage accommodation for its publications at Brighton Museum since 1897 and when this space was no longer available in 1922 they had been

London HQ

transferred to Manchester Museum. The enquiries of Burlington House, and subsequently of the Science Museum, proved to be unsuccessful and although the Library Association itself approached the Association in 1928 on the matter, Council decided to defer any action for the time being.

The Association's membership had remained static for a number of years and in 1927 the Council resolved to send a circular to all non-member museums and to societies likely to be interested in its work. Despite the Association's energies over a wide field, it suffered from an unclear image: it was still perceived as primarily for natural science curators and for the provincial museums and their staff. In an attempt to overcome the former, the words Arts and Sciences were added for a time to the title The Museums Association but it is a moot point whether this created a more apt perception of the organization. The latter was much helped when the British Museum and other London national museums joined in 1930. However, the membership drive successfully increased the numbers from 288 in 1927 to 519 at the end of 1930. Many of the new members were recruited personally by Sir Henry Miers himself, who was to play a vital role in museum affairs over the next decade.

The first regional federation

In 1926 Dr James J Simpson, the Honorary Secretary of the Association, moved from the National Museum of Wales to become Director of the Liverpool Public Museum. It was perhaps understandable that before long he would be thinking in terms of regional co-operation between museums as was being practised through the affiliation scheme of the National Museum of Wales, not that there was nothing novel in professional meetings for museum workers in the north-west of England, as has already been seen in chapter 3. In October of the following year, however, a representative meeting of museum curators was called at the Liverpool Museum and as a result the Federation of Lancashire and Cheshire Museums was formed. The event led the Editor of the Journal to reflect that the type of co-operation now taking place was very much that for which the Museums Association itself was founded. This was the beginning of the development of a country-wide network of regional federations which continue to play an important role in professional exchange today.

Curatorial training

The Welsh Affiliation Scheme had been responsible also for introducing summer schools for museum staff. These started in 1925 and had grown out of the annual conference which it arranged for its members. These summer schools had a strong collection management base with some exhibition training, all of which was organized by the disciplines of the different collection types (Lee 1928). The training of curators had been discussed since the formation of the Association. A full paper on the education of the museum curator was given in 1894 to the annual meeting at Dublin by James Paton (1895). It also formed the subject of the Presidential Address at the Bristol conference by W E Hoyle (1906).

Another paper by Hoyle (1921) on training and diplomas for museum curators at the Winchester conference led to a resolution from the annual business meeting in 1920 asking Council 'to consider the possibility of formulating some scheme of diplomas for museum officials'. When the British Association (1920) report was published shortly afterwards it drew attention to the self-taught, unsystematically-trained provincial personnel and suggested that curators needed a sound training at university and in museum technique. Sir Cecil Harcourt Smith, Director of the Victoria and Albert Museum, was asked by the Association about possible collaboration on training. A statement was made at the next conference that the Council was not yet in a position to make recommendations on a scheme but, after some further correspondence reported to the Executive Committee in September 1921, this line of enquiry seems to have stopped. The issue, however, was not dead and if the comment in the Presidential Address of 1924 is any guide, Council may have been looking to the universities to afford opportunities for curatorial training (Bolton 1924). However, this was not to be for over forty years. A review of the development of professional training has been published by Lewis (1983).

[handwritten margin note: 1960s before formal training introduced]

A Royal Commission

Correspondence in *The Times*, on this occasion concerning an appeal to extend the British Museum (Natural History), again opened up the question of the provincial museums. Bailey (1927), the most persistent of the Association's protagonists for a Royal Commission, responded in the *Journal* pressing for the State to develop a definite policy in regard to museums generally and the relationship between national and provincial museums. Perhaps a solution to the present difficulties might lie in the direction of 'weeding out the national collections and sending the redundant material to those struggling local museums where it is so sorely needed'.

Suddenly, just too late to be discussed at the Association's Isle of Man conference in early July 1927, the Government announced the creation of a Royal Commission on National Museums and Galleries. Its terms of reference were widely defined but they were not precisely what many members of the Association had been seeking. They did not suggest a linking of the national and provincial museums to provide a more cohesive service; local museums were seen only as possible recipients of unwanted specimens. There was a tendency to regard the exhibition of specimens as the main if not quite the only function of a museum, which hardly did justice to the true role of the national institutions. Concern was also expressed at the lack of a representative of the biological sciences among the Commissioners[8] (Museums Association 1927a) and later that the brief did not include the relationship with Commonwealth museums.

If the Association had thought that it might not be asked to provide evidence to the Commission, their fears were quickly dispelled. The Executive Committee was soon to meet, together with some invited past-presidents, to consider its response to such a request. The reply (Museums Association 1927b; Royal Commission on National Museums and Galleries 1928b) dealt with three topics on which specific comment was asked. On the loan of objects from the national institutions, the Association sought that material not required for display or reference be made available, that duplicate material be given or sold to provincial museums, and that the circulation collection of the Victoria and Albert Museum contain more originals and be extended to other museums to embrace the physical and natural sciences and archaeology. The response on fees reveals that at the time the great majority of the provincial museums were free; the Association made it clear that its unanimous view was that this practice should continue and that anything to the contrary restricted their useful-ness in promoting education and entertainment. It was recognized that certain society museums made a charge to meet maintenance costs. As far as the stimulation of public interest was concerned their response was that no general organization existed to promote this. Local action was taken to meet particular circumstances which might involve arranging lectures and demonstrations, liaison with the press, school loan collections, broad-casting, and co-operation with scientific societies or through a 'Friends' organization which might also contribute to purchase funds.

In addition the Association provided its views on two other topics. As far as grants-in-aid for purchases were concerned, it commended the scheme but asked for a change in the conditions in order that the smaller museums might benefit; they were unable to raise the matching funds to qualify for grant. In commenting on assistance from the staffs of the national museums, it spoke of the valued stimulus already existing on a personal basis but sought that this should be encouraged by the controlling bodies of the national museums. The hope was expressed that collaboration might have mutually beneficial results. Five members[9], led by the President, gave oral evidence to the Commissioners. Some of the questions, although not relating to recommendations in the eventual report, nevertheless reflected developments that would in due course follow. For example, the standards required to be eligible for loans from the national collection and the importance of these in encouraging would-be borrowers to improve their accommodation, security and management, and the extension of govern-ment aid to provincial museums for purposes other than the purchase of specimens, were also discussed. Other issues included the advantages of original material rather than reproductions, the desirability of a centralized circulation scheme to cover a wider range of materials, and the allegedly more fragile nature of archaeological material.

The Royal Commissioners issued three reports together with two separate volumes of oral evidence, memoranda and appendices (Royal Commission on National Museums and Galleries 1928a; 1928b; 1929a; 1929b; 1930). The first was an interim report to deal with urgent matters relating to specific museums. They found that, compared with the development of other social services and the expenditure on them, the growth of the national museums had been severely checked and the resulting economies had 'already been pushed beyond the point of prudent administration'. Proposals were also made for extensions or the up-grading of six national museums: the British Museum; the British Museum (Natural History); the Museum of Practical Geology; the National Portrait Gallery; the Science Museum and the Royal Scottish Museum.

The final report appeared in two parts and contained the more general recommendations in which the Association had a particular interest; in general it welcomed the recommendations (Museums Association 1929). The key problems identified by the Commissioners were the passive attitude of the State to museums and the individualistic growth of the national museums themselves. The enlargement of the Victoria and Albert Museum's Circulation Department was recommended, together with other categories of museum material, particularly natural history specimens. The report recognized, however, that the service would be based on material independent of the main collections. They also encouraged the development of loans to other museums, particularly overseas, and recommended new legislation to permit this. As far as the national museums were concerned, a far greater awareness of their visitors was suggested. They were advised to differentiate between the general public and students in their displays and generally extend their contact with schools. The introduction of training for museum staff was also recommended. The Commissioners expressed particular concern at the lack of close formal links between the national and provincial institutions and between the national museums themselves; in this connexion a Standing Commission on Museums and Galleries was proposed which, although advisory, should by its nature and character exercise considerable strength in achieving this. Other recommendations included the development of a National Folk and Open Air Museum and the more active promotion of museums and museum activities generally.

Viewed at the time, the Royal Commission report came at an opportune moment. Apart from kindling public interest itself, it was one of a number of important museum events of the time which was generating increased public awareness and improved opinion on museums: others included the official opening of new buildings for the National Museum of Wales and the Science Museum, a number of important art exhibitions, the important archaeological discoveries of Leonard Woolley at Ur of the Chaldees and the enquiry being undertaken into the provincial museums by the Carnegie

United Kingdom Trustees. By the end of 1930 the Government had announced that a Standing Commission on Museums and Galleries would be set up and the Association sought to be represented on it. Although Sir Henry Miers, the President, was appointed to the Commission, this was not an *ex-officio* appointment (Museums Association 1931b). Another result of the Royal Commission report was the formation of the Conference of Directors of National Institutions to assist in co-ordinating their work. But a downturn in the British economy lay ahead – the deep depression of the thirties. Development involving public-sector monies was likely to be severely restricted.

CHAPTER SIX

FORWARD!

'We are on the eve of possibly the greatest event in the history of the provincial museum movement.' These were the opening words of the Association's President (Bailey 1926) in his address to the Bournemouth conference. He continued 'The Carnegie Trustees . . . are about to finance an enquiry into the work of local museums'. The prediction came true. This was the beginning of a partnership between the Association and the CUKT which was to last for over half a century and was to be a major contributory factor in the great improvement in professional standards and the general public's perception of provincial museums during that period.

In July 1925 the Council resolved that the President and Secretary of the Association should discuss museum development with the Secretary of the Carnegie United Kingdom Trust (CUKT). As a result the Association's Council was asked for its views on the desirability of the CUKT 'preparing and publishing a general report on the public museums of the United Kingdom with special reference to those in smaller centres of population'. Council endorsed the proposal. Following a meeting between the CUKT and representatives of educational and local bodies, who also endorsed it unanimously, the CUKT appointed Sir Henry Miers to to undertake the work. This was an enlightened appointment. Sir Henry was probably better acquainted than anyone else with the state of museums in the United Kingdom. He had served on all the major committees[10] reviewing museum provision since 1913; he was a trustee of the British Museum; he had been aware of the Association's work at least since 1897 when he delivered a paper to the annual meeting. He thus brought an unusually comprehensive perspective to the problem and also bridged the gap between the national and provincial museums. To assist in the museum visiting and in preparing the report an able young man, S Frank Markham, was engaged.

The Carnegie study took under two years to complete. During this period, which also coincided in part with the Royal Commission's investigation (chapter 5), there was a certain expectancy in the air and speculation as to the outcome – building castles in Spain, as the President put it! The Association's work continued to be done on a voluntary basis. Dr Bather who had acted as Honorary Editor for many years was now retiring from his appointment at the British Museum (Natural History) and in August 1927 a young member of staff from the same museum, William E Swinton, accepted the post of Assistant Editor with a view to taking over the editorship in due course; he was to serve the Association in this and many other capacities over a long period of time. In an astute move, the Council invited Sir Henry Miers to become President of the Association for the year 1928–29 by which time his report would be published and he would be in an ideal position to guide and oversee its implementation.

The Miers' Report

The Miers' (1928) report was completed and published earlier than expected and the *Journal* for the following month carried a full review of it by J Bailey (1928a). It was well received but there was an inherent reservation because almost all of its recommendations implied expenditure of a kind not previously available to most museums. This report, taken with that from the Royal Commission, provides a wealth of information about the museums of the British Isles in the late 1920s. The Miers' Report was concerned with the provincial museums of the country; it included art museums but not picture galleries. By its terms of reference it was biased towards services that contributed to education, culture and learning and their possibilities for the future. If this factor had a considerable bearing on a number of the recommendations, it does not seem to have affected the traditional bipartite approach to a definition of museums found at the beginning of the report: 'any building used as a repository for the preservation of objects relating to art, history, science or industry, which is open to the public for the study of these subjects'. So traditional an approach would be more surprising if there were not, elsewhere in the report, further consideration of the purpose of museums: 'their chief function is by means of exhibited objects to instruct, and to inspire a desire for knowledge, children and adults alike; to stimulate not only a keener appreciation of past history and present activities but also a clearer vision of the potentialities of the future'. A further report, prepared by Dr Ernest Lowe (1928b) on his CUKT sponsored visit to review American museum practice, was issued at the same time. A paper on his visit was also presented to the annual conference (Lowe 1928a).

Having found that the 530 museums[11] of Britain were distributed in a very haphazard manner, Miers recommended that a museum should be started in every town with a sufficient population, clearly seeing museums as an educational facility to which all should have access; provision of these was seen as a duty of the local authorities. One museum in each county should be organized to provide, as it were, a county museum service, the report suggested. This would provide the focus for co-ordination and co-operation and the county was seen as the appropriate body to undertake it, particularly as it was the only authority which could hope to provide for the rural population. The county services would include arranging for travelling collections and lecturers for rural areas as well as organizing exchanges and loans between museums and avoiding duplicate collecting. The report noted that about 20% of the local museums received school visits of the type which would be regarded as school attendance, but that only three of them had a specific member of staff responsible for such classes. Only three of the fifty English county education authorities made grants to facilitate such visits. However, the mainly larger museums of the County Boroughs, based on bigger towns, were being used much more by schools although there was little recognition of this by the education authorities in terms of grant.

On the question of collections about 300 museums were of a general character and it is to these more particularly that the report gives closer attention. Many of these miscellaneous collections had started as the original gift to a society or town and the process of accepting almost anything had continued with little attempt to control the process. Every museum, the report recommended, should adopt a definite, restricted collecting policy based on the maximum service that it can render to its own district or county. There is a particular need for local museums to collect objects of local interest, the report states, as well as encouraging regional surveys as were being undertaken at West Ham and Wimbledon. It also draws attention to the need for new types of museum and to the lacunae to be found among certain subjects such as agriculture, hygiene, industry, commerce and naval history collections or, as will be recommended in due course by the Royal Commission, the basis for establishing an open air folk-life museum. In addition to specialist collections there was also a need to collect for specialist audiences such as the blind or for children. On buildings, the report noted that only 10% of the museums reviewed were housed in purpose-built premises and that few of them had storage facilities and workrooms.

On staffing the report painted a particularly poor picture. Only about twelve provincial museums had a full-time competent curator with adequate staff; in more than half of the 530 museums there was no skilled assistance whatever. More than 200 curators combined their post with another responsibility such as librarianship, directing a picture gallery or teaching, for example. The report was particularly critical of 'the disgracefully low standard of salaries', pointing out that on average a curator received about half of that recommended by the Museums Association in 1922 (see chapter 4) and in some cases was paid less than the caretaker; an example was quoted of a city with a population of over 300,000 paying its curator an annual salary of £198 (the recommended minimum was £900). Another factor seemed to have been the lack of any retiring age with the result that there were 'septuagenarian and octogenarian curators, of whom there are a considerable number'.

The evidence for mutual assistance between museums was sparse, the report indicated. Reference was made to the Lancashire and Cheshire Federation's work, the Welsh affiliation scheme and the facilities provided through the Museums Association's conference. On exchanges and loans, the Victoria and Albert Museum's Circulation Department remained the only active facility for the provincial museums. The British Museum's assistance with the identification of specimens was appreciatively noted. The report recommended that the national museums should create an advisory board to promote relations with local museums but went on to state that assistance should only be given to museums which have a definite approved policy towards buildings, purchases and salaries.

The Museums Association was seen as the one form of mutual assistance most capable of being developed quickly and effectively to make an impact on the situation. On the other hand the report was critical – perhaps unduly critical – of its essentially voluntary work:

> The Association can hardly claim to have the full support and confidence of the museums of the country or to have done much except in details to make them more effective; it has been productive of little in the way of better organization or co-operation; it has achieved nothing towards improving the status, salaries and qualifications of curators such as has been done by the Library Association.

The report therefore recommended the strengthening of the Association by increasing its membership, so that it could assist generally in the developments proposed and institute a scheme of museum education.

The first major debate on the Miers' Report was at the Association's conference at Glasgow in early July 1928. A whole morning was devoted to the report which was introduced by a series of speakers (Bailey 1928b; Bather 1928; Bolton 1928; Crowther 1929; Carpenter 1929) each covering different topics in the work. The discussion which followed also considered many aspects of the report but the overriding view was of the accuracy in which the current state of museums had been presented and concern for progress in the matter. Sir Henry Miers closed the proceedings pointing out that the matter now rested with the Carnegie Trustees. He did not know what the outcome would be but, were he a Trustee 'he would feel that the persons most deserving of assistance were those who were endeavouring to help themselves'. Clearly it was now time for the Association to respond. At the conference the following year, Sir Henry Miers (1929), now President, announced at the end of his address that the Association should lend all possible support to start a movement of co-operation on a country-wide basis, that it should have an office in London and employ a paid Secretary and generally reorganize itself, and that it should also issue a new Directory. For the Office, Secretary and the new edition of the Directory an application for a grant had been made to the Carnegie Trustees. A few weeks later the CUKT announced that grant of £1,500 over three years had been awarded to the Association for this purpose.

Incorporation of the Museums Association

In December of that year under the title 'Forward!' the Editor of the *Journal* in jubilant mood announced that Sir Henry Miers had agreed to continue as President of the Association, Frank Markham – who had assisted Sir Henry in his report – had been appointed Secretary and the first permanent home for the Association had been established at 39b Alfred Place, South Kensington. It was now for the Association to reorganize itself for the new role ahead. Attention was given immediately to the legal status of the organization and at the annual meeting in 1930 it was agreed to establish the Association as a Company limited by guarantee. Accordingly a Memorandum and Articles of Association recognizing this were drawn up and from 20 November 1930 these formed the basis of the Association's new legal existence. It was not long before the Association's increased activities severely stretched both its staff and accommodation to the limits. With the promise of an additional grant from the CUKT in 1931, further premises at 26 Alfred Place were leased although the post-box for the Association remained at number 39b. Separate offices were not a satisfactory arrangement and on 25 March 1933 the Association became a tenant of the Library Association in its new headquarters, Chaucer House in Malet Place.

Many other matters exercised Council's mind during this period. The museum use of broadcasting and the cinema, for example, were amongst the issues discussed. Then there was the question of the national open-air folk museum which had been proposed in both the Royal Commission's and the Miers' reports. An editorial on the subject (Museums Association 1930c) announced the creation of a committee to promote the idea, the initiative for which had come from the Royal Anthropological Institute. Supported by a number of national societies, including the Association, the government was approached with a view to establishing such a museum in Regent's Park. The First Commissioner of the Office of Works and the President of the Board of Education jointly set up a committee to examine the matter further and it was hoped to attract private monies to the enterprise (Museums Association 1931a). However, with the deteriorating economic climate, the Committee decided not to proceed on the matter.

But the keyword of the President's clarion call had been co-operation (Miers 1929) and much attention was given to this. In the next ten years most regions of the country would be covered by federations of museums and galleries, but there were other attempts at regional collaboration. An early scheme for county collaboration was proposed in Hertfordshire. Here representatives of the Association and the County Council, together with the Chairmen and Curators of the Hertford and Letchworth museums, met and agreed on archaeological and educational service responsibilities for each of the museums in the county (Museums Association 1931a). However, the representative of the St Albans Museum was not present at the meeting, and when she was unable to attend the next meeting the scheme appears to have gone into abeyance. Another collaborative venture was established in Hampshire where the county's curators commenced meeting twice a year from 1936. Two years later the South-Western Group of Museums and Galleries drew up guidelines on local collecting policies for its members (Wallis 1938) but admitted that the main problem of delimiting a collecting area for each museum appeared insurmountable.

The Standing Commission on Museums and Galleries

Co-operation at a national level came as a result of discussion between the new Standing Commission on Museums and Galleries, the Board of Education and the Scottish Education Department. Following a short study the Board of Education (1931) issued a memorandum on the possibility of increased co-operation between public museums and public educational bodies. This was the first official study that the Board had ever undertaken in relation to the educational role of the provincial museums. Although the leaflet contained a number of suggestions which were impractical or unacceptable professionally, nevertheless it was important, as the editorial in the *Journal* pointed out, because 'we may now expect to have cordial co-operation with Directors of Education and, where expense is involved, the education authorities will now be led to see that it is no less justified than expenditure on sport' (Museums Association 1932a). The pamphlet stated that only about twenty museums in England and Wales were lending exhibits to elementary schools and that some fifty were used for systematic classes with another hundred being visited casually. The formation of circulating collections by museums was encouraged as was the visiting of museums so that original material could be used in teaching. Attention was also drawn to the benefits that the blind and deaf as well as adult audiences could obtain from the handling of specimens.

The Association lost no time, either, in proposing a scheme to the Standing Commission on Museums and Galleries to promote co-operation between the national and provincial institutions. The essence of the proposal was that about twenty of the larger provincial museums should act as an advisory centre for the smaller museums in their region and that the larger museums should provide the link with the national museums. In this way advice could be sought, loans requested, and exchanges and circulating exhibitions arranged; the federations were seen as having an organizational role in the latter arrangements. The Commission replied indicating that the national museums and galleries welcomed participation in any scheme that would foster friendly relations between provincial and national museums but they felt that the present freedom that they enjoyed whereby any museum, however small, had direct access to the national museums should not be lost (Museums Association 1932b). Thus the heart was taken out of the Association's proposal.

Although Sir Henry Miers continued to serve as a Commissioner, theoretically maintaining the link between the two organizations, the benefit to the Association and its members does not seem to have been great. It was not until 1938 that the Commission agreed to establish, at the Association's request and without prejudice to existing *ad hoc* arrangements, an advisory service from the national museums to the provincial museums. Where the expert advisor was not an active member of national museum staff, the costs would be met on a matching basis for the larger museums but with the charge waived in the case of small museums; the Association was asked to advise in the case of museums unable to afford it (Museums Association 1938). As the editorial announcing this noted, 'for the first time the Museums Association has been officially recognized as a unit in the administration of the national museum service in its relations to the provinces'.

CHAPTER SEVEN

HOME AND EMPIRE – THE IMPACT OF CARNEGIE

In April 1930 the CUKT discussed with the Association its planned preliminary experimental work with museums for the period 1931–35; an allocation of £10,000 over the five year period was proposed. Grants on a matching basis would be available for approved work at public museums which had adopted a definite policy as suggested by Miers. In addition grants to assist in curatorial training and for the circulation of museum exhibits in rural areas were being considered. The Executive Committee of the Association examined the proposals in detail and responded positively to the scheme making certain recommendations, particularly on the eligibility of museums for the grant and the conditions that should be attached to it. The proposed CUKT quinquenniel policy for museums was also discussed at the Association's Cardiff conference (Hyslop 1930).

The final scheme, which essentially endorsed the earlier proposal was confirmed in an address to the following annual conference by the Secretary of the CUKT (Mitchell 1932). The grant for small museums was introduced for special outlays such as the purchase of cases or the employment of temporary staff in connexion with a sanctioned reorganization scheme. Each applicant was required to apply to a Joint Committee of the CUKT and the Association and to show that they were prepared to provide adequate annual revenue for the upkeep of the new policy and to have, or be prepared to appoint, a competent curator. Originally the grant was made available on a pound for pound basis with a maximum of £250 for each museum and applied to places with a population between 10,000 and 70,000. However, the number of museums coming forward with proposals was not as great as had been estimated, partly, it seems, because of increasing difficulty to raise the matching funds to attract a CUKT grant. Because of this the population limits were removed in 1934 but additional staffing requirements were required of larger museums. Furthermore the stipulation that the museum be administered by local government was also removed, allowing society museums to apply. Later the maximum grant was increased. Periodic reviews of this aspect of the CUKT policy show that expenditure by the Trust had reached £31,427 by 1945; £80,000 by 1955 and £129,262 by 1965. The Carnegie Trustees continued to maintain a museum policy, although on a reducing scale, until 1975, thus completing half a century of critical aid to museums and museum staff.

CUKT museum development grants

The small museum grants, or museum development grants as they became known, involved first a report on the proposals by an expert named by the Joint Committee with the Association which would be used as the basis to present the scheme to the governing body of the museum. The opportunity to receive an independent development report by a senior museum officer was an important part of the scheme and contributed much to its success. Many of the schemes were concerned with improving the permanent displays and this in turn contributed towards a better public image. The first recipients under the scheme were the museums of Exeter, Lancaster, Letchworth, Newark-on-Trent, Cheltenham and Hereford. Over 250 of these grants were made.

CUKT grants for rural services

The idea of extending existing museum services to the rural population was included in the Miers' Report. Although the CUKT announced their interest in this in 1930, there was no immediate response. In an attempt to stimulate action, and demonstrate what had already been done, the Association and the Trust jointly arranged an exhibition of museum loan service material at the County Hall, London, during a conference of Chief Education Officers but this did not have the desired effect. In 1933 further proposals were drawn up by the Joint Committee which included a paper on town and country museum loan services by W A Smallcombe of Reading. The Trustees made further announcements inviting proposals for rural museum services and again, under the heading 'county museum services', in 1936. In September of that year the CUKT offered a grant of £1,200 to Derbyshire Education Committee to develop a scheme for circulating museum material throughout the county area. This scheme involved the building up of a school loan collection from scratch and maintaining a regular service to Derbyshire schools (Winstanley 1940). Another experimental scheme was also created for Leicestershire, but in contrast this was based on an existing school museums service at Leicester Museum.

CUKT grant for education and training

One way in which the CUKT contributed much to professional develop-ment was in the form of grants to attend courses, meetings and to undertake study tours. This scheme was formally introduced in 1936 to encourage museum staff to undertake visits in this country, on the continent and in the United States. Articles in the *Journal* based on the experiences gained bear witness to the value of these visits. It also enabled junior members of staff to attend conferences and generally to establish professional contact which otherwise would have been impossible. After the formation of the Inter-national Council of Museums in 1946, a number of UK members of museum staff were able to attend its meetings, financed in this way. But perhaps the most important single contribution of all the CUKT grant-in-aid was in its financing of training for museum staff. Although the Association had been discussing training for many years it was only when funding became available from the CUKT to set up and run courses that the scheme came to fruition.

Empire survey and grants

No sooner had the Association begun to establish itself financially, organizationally and professionally that it was looking to completely new areas in which it might operate. The Association had always encouraged overseas membership and many of these members attended the annual conference. As a British institution in the heyday of the Empire it felt close affinities to and responsibility towards the overseas Dominions. In its first separately published directory (Howarth and Platnauer 1911) the Association had included a section on Indian and Colonial museums. It had already agreed that it would publish a second volume of its new directory to include the museums of the Empire. It was in this connexion that Frank Markham approached the Carnegie Corporation of New York for funds. However, it was soon clear that this Corporation had considerable funds at its disposal for work in the British Colonies and the approach for help in publishing a directory soon turned into an application for a general survey of the museum service of the overseas Dominions and Colonies on a similar basis to the survey undertaken by Miers in Britain.

The application for a general survey was successful, the Association being asked to do the work on the understanding that the same team – Miers and Markham – undertook the work; a grant of $30,000 was made to the Association for the purpose. The President, in slightly defensive mood, put this to the annual conference at Plymouth (Miers 1931) and announced that he and the Secretary were planning to visit Canada shortly to carry out 'a complete survey of the Canadian museums'. At the Birmingham conference the following year, Miers (1932) reported that he and Markham had been away from England for two months in Canada and for three-and-a-half months in Africa and that in addition the Honorary Treasurer and the Honorary Secretary had spent seven weeks in the Mediterranean as part of the same mission. Markham had now been invited to undertake the Australian and New Zealand surveys and it was reported to the annual general meeting later in the week that he had resigned as Secretary of the Association.

The survey was completed in 1933 and reports and directories on the museums and art galleries of Australia, New Zealand, Canada, South Africa, Southern Rhodesia, the East African territories, British possessions in the Mediterranean, Ceylon, British Malaya, the West Indies, Fiji, and other colonies were published (Miers and Markham 1932a,b; Miers and Markham 1933a,b; Markham and Richards 1934a,b; Markham and Oliver 1934). As a result of these reports the Carnegie Corporation of New York set aside $263,000 for museum development in various parts of the British Empire, asking the Association to provide the necessary advisory and administrative backup for this grant awarding scheme. Accordingly an Empire Grants Committee was created which was serviced by Frank Markham as Empire Secretary. Conditions for the award of grants were drawn up (Museums Association 1934c) and $54,000 allocated for this. In 1934 funds became available for a survey of the Indian museums and H R Hargreaves was appointed to assist with it. In November 1935 Frank Markham was elected as a member of parliament for the South Nottingham constituency but he was able to see the Indian work completed which was published two years later (Markham and Hargreaves 1936). A separate grant scheme was operated for educational work in the museums of Australia and New Zealand (Museums Association 1936) which was administered by Carnegie from New York. The final report of the Empire Grants Committee (Miers and Markham 1937) gives some idea of the extent of its influence. In 1945 the Carnegie Corporation of New York were asked whether they wished to see the Empire Grants Committee resuscitated but they declined. Frank Markham continued to serve the Association for a time as Honorary Overseas Secretary.

The Diploma

Until 1930 the Association had given much consideration to the training of curators but had taken no action. However, the Miers' Report and more particularly the Royal Commission report underlined the need for training and looked to the Association to take some initiative in the matter. Accordingly the Executive Committee agreed to approach the heads of the national museums for assistance. As a consequence a short course in museum work took place in London from 6–10 October 1930. Of fifty applicants, thirty were taken and they received a mixture of lectures and demonstrations through the week, meeting first in the Science Museum and then in different institutions each day (Museums Association 1930d). The course seems to have been appreciated even if one member, who signed herself 'Knocked-Silly' when writing to the Editor of the Journal about the course, thought it had covered too much ground. The success of the course led to two further courses being planned for 1931, one of two weeks in London and the other of a week's duration in Edinburgh. The CUKT agreed to assist with course expenses, including lecturers' fees and possibly maintenance grants although it was subsequently confirmed that staff from local authority museums could charge authorized expenses to their employers.

At the next Council meeting, W A Gunn of Newport Museum proposed that a sub-committee be formed to consider the provision of training courses including the awarding of diplomas and certificates by the Association. A sub-committee on training course and diplomas was appointed[12] which changed its name to Education Committee at its first meeting. Despite possible confusion with the education function of museums, the Association has always maintained the word 'education' in preference to 'training' in this context. During its deliberations the Committee considered the new Courtauld Institute's proposed degree courses in the history of art and a suggestion from the Wellcome Historical Medical Museum that a three month course in curatorship should be provided in its new premises. However, the Committee persisted with training and a qualification under the control of the Association.

In October 1932 it published regulations for the award of the Diploma of the Museums Association (1932c). These made it clear that while the Association did not regard as its responsibility the provision of knowledge in a relevant academic discipline, it nevertheless required clear evidence of competence in one of these disciplines as well as in 'museum technique' in order to meet the requirements of its Diploma. The Association undertook to offer three courses, each of one week's duration, in order to provide an indication of the standard required: elementary and advanced courses and the third course specialized in a subject approved by the Association. To qualify for the award candidates had to show evidence of competence in an appropriate discipline related to museum collections, take the three courses and successfully demonstrate a competent knowledge of museum administration, methods and techniques, submit a thesis on museum work, and provide an example of their own curatorial work. Before long, additional assessments were required of Diploma students in the form of written examination papers and a practical test (Museums Association 1936). The practical test was replaced by a third, technical paper as a wartime expedient; otherwise it retained this form until 1948. The first Diplomas awarded by examination were presented at the Jubilee Conference in 1939. A useful support to the Diploma students, but intended for the curatorial community as a whole, was the issuing of a series of handbooks for curators (Plenderleith 1933; 1937; Kennedy 1938; North *et al* 1941).

Assistants' Group

It was following a Diploma course in administration, held in Bristol in December 1938, that the idea of an organization for junior museum staff took a positive step towards realization. The idea of establishing a junior membership within the Association had been suggested by Miers (1929). It was given rather more form by W A Gunn of Newport at a Council meeting in June 1932 who suggested that now the Association was providing educational and professional facilities it would be appropriate to form a junior or assistants' section. At the January 1939 meeting of Council a request for assistance in holding a weekend meeting came from the Bristol Diploma course; Council welcomed the principle and offered assistance on the basis of one meeting during the year. This took place in London over the Whitsun weekend. Then followed a request to the Association for official recognition of the Junior Group of the Museums Association but the matter was discussed after the war had started and deferred until the end of hostilities. In November 1944 the idea of an Association of Museum Assistants, affiliated to the Museums Association, was discussed by the Association's General Purposes Committee but it was not until November 1946 that the Museum Assistants Group of the Museums Association was constituted. The group changed its name to the Museum Professionals Group in 1979.

The Markham Report

In 1935 the CUKT agreed to finance a new survey and directory of the provincial museums and galleries of the British Isles. The survey was the responsibility of Frank Markham and the resulting report was published in December 1938 (Markham 1938). It was a logical follow-up to the Miers' Report published ten years previously and in many ways was more balanced in its review of the museum operation. Although Markham's definition of a museum varies from that used by Miers, the statistics presented are broadly comparable. There had been an increase in the number of museums over the previous ten years from 530 to about 800 and Markham added that new 'local museums are now opening at the rate of one every three weeks'. Apart from regimental museums, the most prolific type of museum to develop was the period house or commemorative museum where the associations of an individual or an event had justified the development of the building as a museum. About half of the museums in the British Isles were administered by local authorities; over five hundred of the museums had an annual income of less than £500 a year. The inadequacy of the salaries paid to curators remained much as Miers had found it. On the museum staff themselves he suggested that there was:

a lack of sufficient drive and energy in the museum movement itself.

Much of the slowness of development is due to the fact that the very qualities that go to make up a good curator are often opposed to those that make good reformers. Many curators are so close to their problems that they tend to lose sight of the fact that they are part of a national service. . .

As far as the Museums Association was concerned, the membership had trebled in the ten years but this represented less than 60% of the potential membership. The report also revealed that 110 of the members were from different parts of the Empire and no less than 100 more were from foreign countries. As he said in his report, many of the Association's old problems had been removed but new ones had taken their place; he added that as far as the current position was concerned:

> . . . it is suggested that it is under-staffed and under-financed, and that the normal routine of the business of the Association is such that little time is left over for the hard thinking and constructive investigation which is the first essential of progress.

The overwhelming need for the museums of Britain, as Markham saw it, was for clear direction and authoritative oversight. He reviewed a number of options, including the establishment of a new ministry and the placing of museums under the existing Board of Education. One thing, however, was very clear to him and that was that only the Government could bring long-term direction to the movement. He concluded, however, that a Commission or a Departmental Committee should be the first step to consider the whole question of the future of the provincial museums of this country.

Markham also lists some of the points that he believed should be raised by such a commission: the relationship between the provincial and national museums, bearing in mind the need for greater unity; the grant-aiding by government of the provincial museums and the standards that should be applied to justify this; whether new or existing machinery at the Victoria and Albert Museum should be applied to administer an enlarged grants procedure; how to maintain the independence of museums as far as possible; that the restrictions on co-option to local government committees should be reviewed as far as museum committees were concerned; whether museums might be better administered through a Standing Commission, a Grants Board or some other specially appointed body.

As with its predecessor, half a day was spent discussing the Markham Report at the annual conference. The President of the Board of Education addressed Conference during the week - the first Cabinet Minister to do so - and indicated that although supporting the need for an inquiry into museums the financial position of the country prevented it from being set up immediately. When the Secretary of the CUKT, J Wilkie (1939), spoke he indicated that the Trustees viewed the establishment of an inquiry as the most important recommendation. They had therefore approached the President of the Board who, while giving the answer already heard, might nevertheless be willing to consider an informal inquiry in consultation with the Association and the Trustees. On the question of government grant-in-aid to museums he pointed out that the museum service was established by adoptive legislation and that to date government grant had never been paid to such services. In suggesting government grant with some measure of control, the Markham Report was suggesting something quite revolutionary in library and museum policy. The discussion generally supported the report and a resolution was passed unanimously to this effect, thanking the author for his work. At the close of the debate, Dr Mortimer Wheeler proposed, and conference adopted a resolution calling on the Prime Minister for the establishment of a Royal Commission to investigate the condition and administration of the museums of this country.

This was the Association's Jubilee Conference. A week long, it offered its delegates a very mixed fare. Apart from the important events already described, there were messages of congratulation from the Association's new Patron, Her Majesty Queen Mary, from the International Museum Office, the American and French museums associations, the International Museums Alliance operating in Germany and, of course, the midwife at birth, the Yorkshire Philosophical Society; a number of British organizations also presented congratulatory addresses. There was an afternoon anniversary service at Gloucester Cathedral at the beginning of the conference; a garden party at the country seat of the President, the Viscount Bledisloe who in the introduction to his address gave a brief history of the beginnings of the Association (Bledisloe 1939); a paper by H E Don Salvador de Madariaga (1939), the President of the International Museums Office, on 'Museums and world peace' while Dr Mortimer Wheeler opened a discussion on 'Air raid precautions in museums'. Such a cocktail was but an omen of the gathering storm of another world war.

CHAPTER EIGHT

THE WAR EFFORT...
AND AFTERWARDS

When the Second World War was declared, Britain's curators were slightly more prepared than they had been at the start of the Great War. Indeed in November 1937 the Association's General Purposes Committee had decided to call a conference of museum directors and committee chairmen to discuss the air raid precautions necessary for museums. About 100 people attended the conference from which it was clear that none of the institutions had well-formulated disaster plans for this type of eventuality. The Association was asked to investigate the issue and report at an early date. Independently, but as a result of the meeting, the national museums formed a committee to define and co-ordinate their own air raid precautions and the Association decided to await the published results of this for use in the provinces as well. The President, Dr Mortimer Wheeler who was a member of this committee, did give some sound basic advice on the matter in his address to conference in 1939. However, until the publication of the national museums' committee report (British Museum 1939), it seemed that curators had to rely for their planning on the President's statement, the experience of Spanish curators, published by José Renau, or a publication, mainly concerned with monuments, by Karl F Kühn of Brno.

On 24 August, with the outbreak of war regarded as inevitable, the national museums closed to pack the material of highest importance and transport it to places of considered safety. There was a similar pattern amongst the provincial museums: at Newcastle the Council of the Natural History Society of Northumberland, Durham and Newcastle-upon-Tyne evacuated the most important of the collections in the Hancock Museum to safe locations; at Worthing the local authority museum's fine collection of Saxon glass was packed in a specially constructed metal container and dispatched to a safe location in the Sussex countryside. The *Journal* for the first few months of the war reported on museum closures and openings and cases where museum and gallery buildings had been requisitioned for other purposes; the Walker Art Gallery at Liverpool, for example, was used to house food and fuel offices.

The aerial bombardment, expected immediately, did not materialize for about a year. When it came, however, museums were soon among the casualties. On one night alone, 8 September 1940, three of the London museums were damaged in air raids; the following month the British Museum had the remarkable experience of two bombs on different days passing through the same hole in the roof; neither exploded (Forsdyke 1941). Other bombs caused considerable damage. The Victoria and Albert Museum, for example, was damaged in April 1941 and had to close for a few days but, apart from a three-month closure in 1944 because of blast damage, the Museum remained open for most of the War. The damage to museums was not confined to London. The pages of the *Journal* reveal that Birmingham, Bristol, Hull, Liverpool, Manchester, Sheffield, to name a few of the larger museums, had been damaged, some of them very badly. An indication of the extent of the war damage on museums and galleries can be gained from the list in Markham (1948). The Museums Association's offices did not escape either: on two occasions in 1941 the building was damaged, in one of these a porter and the cleaner were quickly on the scene to limit the damage and the Council presented them both with cheques for their swift action.

Council met a few days after the outbreak of war and determined a number of policy issues. Frank Markham, who had been elected President of the Association in 1939, was asked to continue in office, with Sir Cyril Fox deputizing for him as necessary; it was confirmed that the CUKT grant to maintain the Association's office would continue and there was agreement that the Association should maintain the London office normally as far as possible although some revision of office hours was necessary to accommodate blackout regulations. If it became necessary, there was the possibility of moving the office to Cheltenham, the home of the Honorary Secretary, although the Yorkshire Federation had also offered assistance. Council's policy on museums during the War was clearly stated from the outset in two war circulars issued to members (Museums Association 1939a,b), namely wherever possible to continue existing services, provide additional educational services for which grant was available (Museums Association 1940b) and assist the war through exhibitions and other media. On the latter point some reservation was expressed by Sir Cyril Fox about the use of museums for purely propaganda purposes. The Association subsequently arranged exhibition tours of war artists' work and also provided assistance to the Ministry of Information in their scheme for circulating photographic exhibitions to museums and galleries (Museums Association 1940c).

Except for 1944, the annual general meeting was held in London during the war and without an associated conference. This meant that the *Journal* was the main point of contact for members although meetings of the federations continued mainly to take place. Local government employees over the age of 25 were considered to be in reserved employment and not therefore subject to national service in the forces, but a number did join up and some museums became depleted of staff. However, when the Government announced the dereservation of museum staff in April 1941, Council decided to protest on behalf of those staff who were over military age and in the case of others where the closing of the museum would follow. Similarly some members of Council, including the President, enlisted. In 1941 the Secretary of the Association was appointed to a post in the Petroleum Department which enabled him to continue the oversight of the Association's office for a time, but eventually other arrangements were necessary and a member of the Secretariat, Mrs Bond, maintained the office for the rest of the war. In thanking her, members of Council indicated that had it not been for her work, the Association would have been unable to maintain a London office through the War. There was a slight interregnum before T H Rowsall took up the post of Secretary-Editor in 1946.

The Association's financial position also deteriorated, dependent, as it was, on subscription income. In 1942 the *Journal* was reduced in size to help meet the Association's finances and the following year the CUKT, who had already made an advance so that the Association need not sell its investments, indicated that they would provide a guarantee of up to £500 per year on any reasonable deficit that the Association might incur for the duration of the war. The *Journal* size was, however, further reduced in 1943 in response to the Government's control of paper order. Because of the paper shortage, the General Purposes Committee had already agreed that all copies of the annual report prior to 1940 and all but 30 reserve copies of pre-war journals should be put to salvage. Another understandable government economy was on fuel. On this the Association organized a deputation to the Ministry of Fuel with the national museums to obtain special concessions so ensuring that museum objects were maintained in reasonable temperatures.

Post-war reconstruction

Just before war had been declared, the Association's conference had received a major report on the state of the non-national museums and had passed a resolution calling for the appointment of a Commission to investigate the problems that they faced. In January 1940, the President wrote to the President of the Board of Education arguing that the time was opportune for a commission to undertake the required review. The President of the Board replied in negative terms (Museums Association 1940). This was reported to the Council who asked that a revised memorandum be prepared on the subject and recirculated for comment. The Secretary of the CUKT advised on further amendments and suggested that the matter would be better left for the time being. The memorandum, and more importantly the report that gave rise to it, however, had a more immediate purpose. As a result of enquiries by the Association in 1941, it was invited by the Greenwood Committee – a sub-committee of the War Cabinet – to submit proposals for the post-war reconstruction of museums and galleries. The federations were consulted and a committee established[13] by Council to undertake the work.

This memorandum went through a number of revisions, the last of which was undertaken by Mr Christopher Hawkes, and this was published in the *Journal* (Museums Association 1942). It owed much to the Markham Report and after clearly stating the functions of museums, drew attention to the financial and administrative needs of museums, emphasizing their local character and educational role. This memorandum formed the basis for a deputation to the Ministry of Reconstruction[14]. However it is clear that Council was still not satisfied with the memorandum. The President devoted the whole of his address to the issue of a long-term plan for museums (Allan 1943) and then a further statement was made in the *Journal* (Museums Association 1943). It is also clear from the minutes of Council early in 1944 that an extended memorandum was to be prepared and, subsequently, that two memoranda were amalgamated by Dr F J North. S D Cleveland (1951) in his presidential address six years later implied that there was also an art gallery committee as well, although there is no record of one being formed in the Association's minutes. This would, however, be perfectly consistent with the form that the memorandum eventually took (Museums Association 1945).

The new version developed Markham's recommendation for a national body concerned with all museums into a Museum and Art Gallery Grants Board, modelled on the old University Grants Committee. The Board would have two sections, one concerned with museums and the other with galleries, the latter being intended to take over the responsibilities of the Council for the Encouragement of Music (CEMA) which had been established at the beginning of the war with the aid of the Pilgrim Trust. It was intended that the Board would assess new schemes, define standards and allocate grant under the control of an inspectorate. Finance, which had a high priority in the document, would be available for both revenue and capital expenditure. In the event the Arts Council of Great Britain was established after the war to provide many of the art functions of CEMA. No parallel body was created to help co-ordinate, finance and assist museums and galleries in their established role. At the close of the War some museums approached the Association, for example Southampton and Aylesbury, seeking development reports to assist in the post-war redevelopment and the Association was pleased to recommend members to act as consultants for this purpose.

International reconstruction

As the War drew to a close, reconstruction of the international community commenced. The old League of Nations had ceased to exist. Some of its associated bodies continued a little longer, the International Museums Office until 1946 contributing as a final publication to the problem of reconstruction (Foundoukidis 1945); a short account of its work was published in the *Journal* (Museums Association 1945). The United Nations system replaced this. In October 1945 the Association was invited to send a representative to the Meeting of Allied Ministers of Education, called to discuss the formation of Unesco. Dr Douglas Allan attended. With the establishment of Unesco in 1946 the Association was asked to nominate members to the national co-operating body. Messrs Lambert and Cleveland were named to represent arts and literature and Drs North and Wallis as delegates to the science and museums group.

The question of an international non-governmental body representing museums was also discussed with the Association during a visit to Britain by Mr Chauncey J Hamlin, President of the Buffalo Museum of Science and a past-president of the American Association of Museums. An International Council of Museums (ICOM) had been formed and each of the European countries visited by Mr Hamlin was invited to set up a national committee. A British national committee was created[15] and in its early days, the Association fostered it as one of its own committees. The first meeting of ICOM was held in Paris in November 1946 and a delegation[16] attended from Britain; three of them were appointed to the ICOM Executive Committee: Sir John Forsdyke as a Vice-President with Leigh Ashton and Frank Markham as committee members. When it came to organizing the ICOM General Conference in London in 1950, the Association was closely involved. A grant of £500 was received from the Ministry of Education to assist with the organization and the CUKT contributed a matching sum to enable the Association to provide a reception for the delegates at Kenwood. In 1952 the Association assisted ICOM in a membership drive in the Commonwealth; when an international museums week was held four years later the Association again did much to promote it.

Internal reconstruction

There was, however, the case of the reconstruction of the Association itself. Among the first items for action was the re-establishment of contact with the government regarding the promised commission to examine the provincial museums and galleries. An approach made early in 1946 for a deputation to meet the Financial Secretary to the Treasury failed, but contact was established with the Labour Party's Art and Amenities Group, and for a time its Chairman, Dr Barnet Stross, was co-opted to the Association's Council. A meeting with the Chancellor of the Exchequer did ensue, from which the possibility of government grant for provincial museums, channelled through the Ministry of Education, began to appear a reality. However, legislation would be necessary for this to come to fruition. At about this point the South-Eastern Federation passed a resolution stating that any future legislation should ensure the autonomy of museums and should not be controlled by education authorities. However, in 1949 discussions on an amending Education Bill were underway with the possibility of a central fund of £250,000 for dispersal. But an election was looming, to be followed by a short parliament, a change of government, increasing financial restraint and dissention from a minority of local authorities over the scheme; together these conspired to prevent further progress.

And then there was the CUKT grant scheme. A few grants had been made during the war years but a new quinquennium commenced in 1946 and the Trustees allocated £30,000 for museum and art gallery development. The grants continued to be administered by a Joint Committee of the Trustees and the Association and were available for the commissioning of expert reports on museums, for museum reorganization and development, for training and assistance with travel and this broad pattern continued into the 1960s. But if there were monies to encourage museum development, there was also concern that a number of museums, damaged or requisitioned during the war, had not re-opened. For example, the Rochdale Museum was still occupied by the Ministry of Food in 1947 and Dr Stross raised the matter in the Commons on behalf of the Association. This general issue was still alive six years later when the Association wrote to the Town Clerk of Liverpool and the Minister for Housing and Local Government emphasizing the need to restore the war-damaged museum completely.

The Association's Diploma scheme was also returned to its full strength; more exacting standards to bring the scheme nearer to new post-war requirements were soon introduced by the new Chairman of the Education Committee, Dr F J North, with revised regulations being approved by the Annual General Meeting in 1948. He commenced work in 1946 on providing opportunities for technical staff to qualify but it was not until 1954 that a Technical Certificate was introduced, based on assessment in the candidate's own museum after not less than five years' experience. About this time the National Joint Industrial Councils for Local Authorities (Scotland) formally recognized the Association's Diploma for promotion purposes and a few years later it was reported that the Burnham Committee had listed it as a degree-equivalent when combined with two years teaching experience. In 1955 there were discussions on the availability of the training for overseas candidates. The Secretary of State for Colonial Affairs had circulated all colonial governments with details of the Association's Diploma. However, the Museums Association of Australia had already decided to proceed with its own scheme but no less than fourteen South African students registered with the Association. 1956 saw the introduction of tutors to assist those home students that requested them.

The question of a Royal Charter had, of course, been considered before but the Cardiff meeting in 1948 returned to it briefly, if only to agree after much discussion that this was not yet the time to seek such recognition. It decided however that the Memorandum and Articles of Association needed revision. Accordingly, the following year a draft was put to the annual meeting on the basis that the final revision would come forward next year. This was agreed but there began a long and spirited debate on the voting rights of institutional members which was to continue into the following year in the form of whether institutional members should have a seat and voting rights on Council. On this point the new constitution was rejected. Council immediately called together an informal committee of institutional representatives and senior members of Council to look at the issue and recommended to Council that its number should include three institutional members in future. An amendment on this was lost and so the new Articles of Association with the revised composition of Council went to the annual meeting and were passed with only three dissenting votes. It was noted in the Council minutes in July 1952 that the institutional representatives had had a meeting during the conference to discuss annual meeting business and that this would become an annual requirement. The overall consequences of the changes were considerable, not least that the Association would in future award associateships and fellowships as a category of membership, in common with many professional bodies; the invidious task of classifying members into the new categories of membership fell to a Classification Sub-Committee whose recommendations were duly approved by Council. These new benefits also attracted additional members and by 1953 the membership had topped 1,000 for the first time.

Trusts and Funds

The Association received a gift and a bequest of money during this period which commenced two of the funds now available to members. The first of these, the Benevolent Fund, commenced from an anonymous gift of £100 in January 1953 to start a 'President's Fund' for past or present professional members of the Association or their immediate dependents who might be in financial distress. The donor was later identified, with his consent, as Sir Frank Markham. The capital was invested and with other contributions from members over the years has proved a important source of assistance. In 1959 the Association was informed that Walter Beecroft, a retired solicitor living in Southend-on-Sea, was bequeathing the residue of his estate to the Association. This was to be used to assist museums in the purchase of pictures and works of art not later than the end of the eighteenth century. The legacy, totaling £17,000, was passed to the Association in 1961. A further bequest, in memory of Daphne Bullard, was received in 1973 to promote the work of textile and costume conservation, display and publication (Bullard 1974). The Association had received other small bequests in the past – for example from Lord Sudeley and Sir Henry Miers – but, unlike some other national organizations, never benefited from a major endowment.

Legislation

A number of issues relating to legislation or its application demanded the Association's attention during this decade. The export controls relating to works of art recurred a number of times. This was at the time when the Waverley (1952) Committee were determining criteria on which the withholding of export licences might be based. The Association contributed to its work and afterwards were asked to nominate eight representatives of non-grant-aided museums and galleries to the Advisory Council for the Export of Works of Art. With an assurance that provincial museums were eligible to bid for material on which export licences were being temporarily withheld, the Association asked for notification of the material as it became available. However, when this started in 1956, the Secretary received only thirty-six hours notice during which a decision had to be made. This was clearly unworkable and longer notice was sought. In 1960 the Association attempted to prevent the export of the painting *Holy Family* by Rubens for the benefit of a provincial gallery; an appeal was launched through the *Journal* and one month later it was announced that Liverpool had purchased it, an unprecedented matching government grant of £25,000 having been paid (Nightingale 1960a,b).

On the question of works of art being given in settlement of death duties, the Association expressed concern to the Treasury in 1953 that State museums always benefited from this arrangement. They responded, pointing out that under the current Finance Act material could be held in the area of its origin. Council also discussed the sale of museum collections as a result of the debate linked with the passage of the *National Gallery and Tate Gallery Act 1954* through parliament which expressly prevented the Trustees from selling any item from their collections. The Council also reviewed three local Bills that contained museum provisions. The Leicester Corporation Bill 1955 contained a clause permitting an admission charge at a proposed folk museum and the Leeds Corporation Bill the following year also sought to sanction charges. This was opposed by the Association in both cases although the final Acts allowed charges to be made. Dr David Owen challenged the justification for the view on admission charges expressed by Council on behalf of the members and indicated that he would put a resolution on the matter to the next general meeting. Before the Association had had an opportunity to express a collective view, however, the Halifax Corporation Bill 1959 was before parliament with a similar provision. In this case no opinion was given by Council in view of 'varying local circumstances'. The question of accumulative purchase funds for municipal museums was also discussed and Sir Frank Markham and Dr

Barnet Stross were both approached on the matter. Legislation in 1964 eventually overcame this problem.

The 1950s commenced somewhat presumptuously with the Festival of Britain in 1951, with which the Association does not seem to have involved itself. The reality of the decade is far more of severe financial restraint. The 1952 conference at Oxford, for example, passed a resolution condemning the government's reduction of the national museums' vote by £30,000, a motion which originated from the South Midlands Federation. The same year the South African Museums Association wrote suggesting that the Association in Britain should change its name to avoid confusion, the Museums Association of the British Commonwealth being suggested. The matter was considered by Council who decided to take no action. Then it was reported that the BBC had approached the Association about a possible television programme, 'Animal, Vegetable, Mineral?' but had proceeded without further contact. The programme involved a panel of experts who were challenged by a museum to identify a group of objects from their collection. It did much to place museums and their collections in a different light. The 'star' of the programme was Sir Mortimer Wheeler, a past-president of the Association.

In 1954 the Association looked at its long-term priorities and decided that its should first see established a technical service for smaller museums and then attempt to provide a permanent headquarters in London with club facilities for its members. In fact change was already in the air. The Secretary-Editor, G P Griggs, left the Association for a senior publishing appointment and was replaced by Michael Nightingale who served the Association from 1954–60. The problem of accommodation was also acute. The Association had left Chaucer House in 1948, when the Library Association needed more space and had taken rented accommodation in Exhibition Road. Council's attention was now directed to a property at 33 Fitzroy Street which would serve the Association's needs in the short-term but which also offered to be a very good investment. After considerable negotiation by the Association's new Secretary, it was purchased in January 1955 for £3,750. The Association still owns the premises which became important collateral for it at one difficult stage. It was used as a head-quarters, however, for about six years; the Association then moved, in 1962, to 87 Charlotte Street. With the appointment of Philip James as Secretary-Editor in 1960, the *Museums Journal* was changed from volume 61 to a quarterly periodical in order to print more substantial papers. At the same time a monthly *Bulletin* was introduced for members. Both carried the armorial bearings of the Association which had recently been granted. These publications continued until 1989 when the two were combined to provide a monthly publication once again. Other Association publications of the 1950s include the *Handbooks for Curators* series and the annual *Museums Calendar*, now known as the *Museums Yearbook*. A series of information sheets were issued later.

Royal patronage

The Association had enjoyed the royal patronage of Queen Mary from 1938 until her death in 1953. There was considerable delight when it was announced in 1955 that Her Majesty Queen Elizabeth the Queen Mother had graciously consented to become Patron of the Association, which it has enjoyed and deeply appreciated since that date. In 1955 it was proposed that King Gustav VI Adolf of Sweden be awarded the Honorary Fellowship of the Association which he accepted. The President and Secretary visited Stockholm on 26 September 1955 to present the certificate of fellowship and copies of the Association's publications to the King.

Help for the small museum

With a slightly easing economic climate, the Association again looked at ways in which government grant-aid might be provided to ease the plight of the smaller provincial museums. A memorandum was completed early in 1954 as a basis for discussion with the Association of Municipal Corporations but as they had not responded nearly a year later, a new approach was taken involving the CUKT and the Arts Council. A further memorandum was prepared based on the idea of an independent Museum Grants Committee and Sir Kenneth Clark discussed this with the Chancellor of the Exchequer. At this point a telling example of the problem that the Association had been fighting for so long came to public notice. The Trustees of the Bowes Museum at Barnard Castle announced that they would have to close the Museum from 30 September 1955 for lack of funds. The Association was much involved in the negotiations which eventually led to the Durham County Council taking over responsibility for it.

Sharpened by the reality of the situation, a memorandum was prepared for the Chancellor of the Exchequer seeking an immediate fund to assist small museums as an interim measure but reiterating the need for a Royal Commission. The CUKT generously offered £25,000 if the government would provide not less than £50,000. In due course the Association of Municipal Corporations and the National Institute for Adult Education joined in the support for the proposals; Sir Philip Hendy and Sir George Dyson addressed a group of MPs on the subject. Some agreement seemed at last to have been reached when Sir David Eccles agreed to give some grant while declining to set up a Royal Commission. He was, however, almost immediately replaced in office and the position became unclear.

A new factor had entered the arena by mid-1957: regionalization. This was debated at the Bristol conference; some of the principles of self-help proposed were not new (see, for example, Hodge 1947; 1949). However, the idea of a regional museum service was discussed with the Parliamentary Secretary for the Ministry of Education who indicated that the support of the local authority associations would be vital before the government would consider a proposal on these lines. The Association's strategy was now based on the idea of regional museum services and on 23 September 1957 an invitation was issued to a meeting on a proposed regional museum service for the south-west. The meeting set up a steering committee to investigate and report back. The idea progressed and with some subscriptions, totalling £400, it was agreed to proceed with technical appointments if funding could be found. The CUKT did not feel able to support the scheme; an even greater disappointment arose when the government declined to assist. However, the Association of Municipal Corporations strongly supported it and wrote to their members urging support. Then three grants from the Gulbenkian, Dulverton and Pilgrim Trusts arrived and the scheme became a reality (Nightingale 1957; Wheeler 1957).

CHAPTER NINE

FORWARD AGAIN!

No one would have considered, in those difficult early days of the embryonic regional museums service for the south-west, that the Standing Commission on Museums and Galleries would be the agency through which the provincial museum movement would at last move forward again. On its past record, the Commission's very limited contact with the provincial museums had been mainly in connexion with the work of the Circulation Department of the Victoria and Albert Museum. Further, Sir George Dyson, Chairman of the Carnegie Trustees, had unsuccessfully sought the Commission's support in 1958 for government aid to the provincial museums (Carlisle 1987) and the Association had been equally unsuccessful with a deputation to the Commissioners early in 1960 when seeking aid for the south-west scheme.

In fact the Chancellor of the Exchequer had written to the Chairman of the Standing Commission, the Earl of Rosse, on 2 March 1960 inviting the Commission to undertake a review of the provincial museums; a meeting of the Commission on 21 April agreed to this unanimously and appointed a sub-committee to undertake the work (Carlisle 1987). In the press announcement made in June, the following terms of reference were given:

> To ascertain the scope, nature and significance of the local collections, the manner in which they are organised, the resources available to them and the possibilities of their further development on a basis of regional co-operation.

This, to a considerable extent, met the Association's contention, which it had promoted ever since Markham's call for a Royal Commission in 1938, for a thorough examination of the provincial museum scene. Without detailed information it was difficult for the Association to argue the case; it was equally difficult for government to justify any action it might take. The Association had started a survey of provincial museums from its own resources; it now passed this information to the Commission and awaited its findings.

By this time there was increasing evidence of public interest in museums.

69

At a political level both of the major parties had implied a brighter future for museums in their recent leaflets on leisure; the link with leisure was to become increasingly significant. There was a boom in museums, as an article in the *Observer* put it, when discussing the large London museums: 'business is booming and the museums are crowded with ordinary people genuinely interested in what the museum has to offer', it stated. Commenting on this, Loraine Conran (1961) said in a *Journal* editorial 'museums throughout the country have been experiencing an increase in popular interest for more than a decade'. The publication of another political pamphlet early in 1963, *Government and the Arts* by the Conservative party then in power, gave some encouragement in that it referred to 'relatively modest grants' for the Area Councils. Another suggestion in the pamphlet was for arts spending to be transferred from the Treasury to the Ministry of Public Buildings and Works (later to become the Department of the Environment). An editorial on this (Museums Association 1963) looked briefly at the relative merits of this against transfer to the Ministry of Education or to a 'Ministry of Fine Arts' which, it said, 'has hitherto been treated with suspicion and indeed repugnance'.

The Rosse Report

The report of the Standing Commission (1963) was published in good time for a full debate at the Newcastle conference (Rosse *et al* 1963). The conference was addressed by the Minister for Education, Sir Edward Boyle, and spokesmen from the Conservative and Labour parties contributed to the debate on the Rosse Report. Support came from both parties and from the conference as a whole. The report contained an analysis of some 876 provincial museums and galleries which included details of their collections, funding and administrative arrangements as well as the salary of the senior museum officer for each one. Many of its recommendations echoed those of earlier reports but others were new. On the question of acquisitions, local authorities running art galleries should be permitted to accumulate funds for the occasional outstanding purchase and provision should be made to remove the legal restraints of forming capital funds for purchases. It called for the grant-in-aid fund of the Victoria and Albert Museum for purchases by the provincial museums to be increased from £25,000 to £200,000 a year for the next five years and then to be reviewed; the Royal Scottish Museum fund should also be increased proportionately. On the question of the travelling exhibitions organized by the Victoria and Albert Museum, expansion of staff and facilities was supported to increase this programme to the provinces and similarly for other national museums, particularly the British Museum and the Science Museum, to provide such a service.

Particular attention was paid to staffing. The report recommended that every museum should have at least one paid officer, that adequate qualifications should be sought and appropriate salaries be paid to all museum staff. On training the government was asked to grant-aid the Association both to provide an Education Officer and to set up a training institute which would provide in-service training towards a professional diploma, technical and craft certificates. The national and larger provincial museums were asked to employ students as trainee assistants. The report reiterated the recommendation of the Roberts Report on public libraries that, in future legislation, the powers governing libraries should be dealt with separately from those relating to museums and galleries. On buildings there was strong support for museum development, particular attention being drawn to the urgency of preserving agricultural, scientific and industrial objects. The sharing of financial responsibility for museums between local authorities was also recommended.

In accordance with the terms of reference requiring the survey to examine the collections and the resources available to them, the report lists the collections classified by subject and then makes a number of recommendations about them. For archaeology it suggests greater co-operation between local museums and government services involved in excavation and suggests that at least one museum in each area should be fully equipped to take on responsibility for such work. On the question of natural history collection, co-operation between local and national museums is recommended and the report supports the idea of type specimens normally being kept at the British Museum (Natural History). The possibility of ethnography collections in small museums being brought together in a central store for loans and exhibitions is stated as is the desirability of regiments passing their collections to local civilian museums. The report also emphasized the need for school museum services to be established country-wide, especially loan services for the rural areas and also for teacher training officers to be appointed in each area. Attention was also drawn to the social facilities that museums could provide.

But the fundamental recommendation of the report was that all local authorities should join with other local authorities and voluntary organizations maintaining museums in their area with a view to preparing a co-ordinated scheme for museum development. There was a minor quibble in the conference debate whether the word 'co-ordinated' should not have read 'co-operative' but an important key to the ready acceptance of the report was the fact that the government had, albeit hurriedly, allocated £10,000 towards the development of the area schemes. In addition, by this time there were Area Councils with appointed staff in the south-west, the Midlands and the north of England with coverage for the rest of the country underway. The Association was already involved with the Standing Commission in setting up the machinery for the administration of the Area Council scheme. The full story of their development can be found elsewhere (Standing Commission 1967; Museums & Galleries Commission 1984; Harrison 1971).

The Rosse Report recommendations directly affecting the Association, namely in the provision of an Education Officer and the creation of a training institute did not receive government support. This was a blow to the Association, not only because the opportunity of developing its training had been frustrated but because this would have relieved the Association of an expense it had borne for many years, albeit with the generous assistance of the CUKT. The CUKT, however, was gradually withdrawing its grant after so many years of aid, and the Association was having financial difficulties. It had substantially raised subscriptions in 1961 but this did not generate the income needed and the Association was in deficit again for the year 1963–64. Staff costs had necessarily to be reduced and the Secretary, Philip James, took retirement to alleviate the position. The Assistant Secretary, Brenda Capstick, became Acting Secretary for a year and in May 1965 took over as Secretary of the Association, a post she held for eighteen years; she was awarded the OBE in 1976 for her services to the Association. Like her predecessor, Philip James, she also received the distinction of election to Honorary Fellowship of the Association.

The Association's financial fortunes at this time were at variance with the national trend which was of relative prosperity, bringing with it museum development. The number of vacancies advertized in the *Bulletin* began to rise significantly. The Victoria and Albert Museum grant-in-aid for provincial museum and gallery purchases was doubled in 1964 to £50,000 and in the following year to £100,000. It was the time of the publication of Jennie Lee's white paper *A Policy for the Arts: The First Steps* – from which, irrelevantly, museums and galleries became linked with the 'dead arts'. New legislation for the local authority museums in England and Wales – the *Libraries and Museums Act 1964* – reached the statute book (Edwards 1965), although with little or no input from the Association or regard to the recommendations of the Roberts and Rosse reports. Rightly or wrongly, museum staff were looking outside of their immediate environment for development opportunities: greater participation in rescue archaeological work (Barton 1974); involvement in biological distributional studies (Spalding 1966); greater awareness of the industrial heritage and on-site preservation (Hudson 1965). These were indicators of change.

They can equally be found within the Association. This was a period in which a number of new issues begin to assert themselves and which would influence the 1970s and beyond. The 1964 conference, unusually, did not have a curatorial theme: it was concerned with museum public relations. This was the time of the introduction of new regulations for the Diploma of the Association and also the commencement of the University of Leicester's Department of Museum Studies in which the Association had been closely involved (Singleton 1966). The appearance of small independent museums was now significant enough for the Yorkshire Federation to move a resolution to the effect that the Association should not encourage these unless there was sufficient regular income to pay a full-time curator. The strongly educational theme of the Glasgow conference was the first step towards the statement on museums in education which the Association published in 1971. The resolutions from the Sheffield colloquium on information retrieval for museums (Lewis 1967) saw the formation of the Information Retrieval Group of the Museums Association (IRGMA), the precursor of the Museum Documentation Association (MDA). The paper by Francis Cheetham (1966) entitled 'Towards a national museum service ?' was the first statement that led in due course to the Association's policy statement on the issue.

The concept of a national museum service was not in itself new. Rather it was a development of a number of notions, topical at the time: governmental regional planning as a national framework; the reorganization of local government; a concern that the Area Museum Councils were providing a face-lift for the small museums but not tackling the real problems affecting larger museums to which was related general concern about museum standards (Cheetham 1968; Atkinson 1968; Owen 1969). The Association submitted evidence to the Royal Commission on Local Government taking the view that the museum service in the provinces should be based on larger administrative units and, another factor of concern to the Association, that regional commitments undertaken by existing museums should be developed and given financial recognition. The Council of the Museums Association (1968) also prepared a statement of policy on local government reform following the publication of the Maud and Mallaby reports on the management and staffing, respectively, of local government. In this it reiterated the need for properly qualified curators with direct access to the governing committees on the policy and executive aspects of their museums. At the Liverpool conference in 1970 delegates heard papers on the Redcliffe-Maud and Wheatley reports concerning local government reorganization in England and Wales and in Scotland and also received a working paper 'A museum service for the nation: the case for state help for selected major museums throughout Great Britain'. The following year the annual general meeting approved Council's revised document on the subject, confirming the principle of a regional museum service with certain 'national museums in the provinces'.

The Exeter conference also dealt with a number of other matters of deep professional concern. Charging for admission to museums arose again because the government had announced suddenly in October 1970 that it was introducing entry fees to the national museums and galleries. The Association undertook a survey of its members on the issue, publishing the results in the *Bulletin*; there was a clear majority of professional opinion against charging. A resolution from the Museum Assistants Group opposing charging was also reported to the conference (Johnston 1971). In fact, for legal and other reasons, the charges were not introduced until January 1974, and then lasted for only three months. The conference also received papers on the disposal of museum objects; the Association had endorsed the Cottisloe Report (1964) at the time but attention was now drawn to recent sales from British collections. A voluntary scheme for accrediting museums was approved; this had been discussed as a register of museums at the 1969 conference but now followed the model developed in the United States more closely although, unlike it, the British scheme was not to prove a great success (Thompson 1982).

The Wright Report

The next governmental report on provincial museums and galleries was prepared by the Department of Education and Science (1973). Chaired by C W Wright, it included representatives of the Association, the Standing Commission, the national museums and the local authority associations[17]. It was appointed to review the needs, particularly of conservation and display, of the principal local museums and galleries and to make recommendations for improving the inter-relationship between these and the national museums with particular reference to specialist services. Lord Eccles (1973) presented the report to the annual conference at Dundee. Amongst its many recommendations were far-reaching proposals for a new structure to accommodate and co-ordinate the provincial museum scene. This was based on a central body which would advise central and local government on museum policy, argue the case for resources and channel funds to the provincial museums according to a considered plan. At a regional level, provincial museum councils were to continue and expand the existing work of the area museum councils. At a local level, a limited number of museums, or groups of museums, would become 'provincial centres of excellence' which would provide services to other museums and so improve standards of provision.

This aspect of the report was particularly topical with the impending reorganization of local government. In his presentation, Lord Eccles (1973) suggested that this was the moment to get the provincial museum structure right for the opportunity of such a reorganization 'will not recur for a long time'. In fact most of the local authorities had already made their decisions and in many cases new arrangements were operating in parallel with the existing services. An 'housing the museums fund', recommended in the report, was rejected by Lord Eccles but otherwise the report was never debated or acted upon by parliament.

Local Government reorganization

The Association lobbied strongly for museums to be a first-tier responsibility during the passage of the Local Government Bill through parliament. In the end museums and galleries became a concurrent function, exercisable by Counties and Districts in England and Wales, with a similar situation in Scotland although the position of the Regions was slightly stronger in that they had responsibilities to ensure the adequate provision of services in each of their constituent Districts. Although a number of authorities amalgamated, so bringing some museums together under common management at a District level, there was little transfer of museums to the first tier authorities except at Leicester, Liverpool and Norwich where county services were created; subsequently the Tyne and Wear County Service was formed. However, many members continuing to operate in small units found themselves operating within other departments, for example, education, recreation or leisure. From an Association viewpoint, as Cheetham (1974) said, a 'unique opportunity has largely been allowed to slip away'. There were, however, some benefits (Loughbrough 1978). It was a period of expansion for museums. Some county councils set up museum services from scratch; existing museums were rationalized with some new posts, particularly to provide museum services; staff salaries improved in some cases as they were brought into line with other services with which they were now operating or because of increased responsibilities.

But local government reorganization actually took place at the beginning of an economic decline which was to intensify and continue well into the 1980s. In fact the *Journal* carried an article on the economics of museum and galleries that year (Peacock & Godfrey 1974). In an editorial, Max Hebditch (1974) commented on the museum as a firm, the winning of the Museum of the Year Award by a museum business, the National Motor Museum at Beaulieu, and the fact that Lord Montagu was predicting that a one pound admission charge would be acceptable to the public in the not too distant future. By 1979, the conference was looking at the value of museums to the economy (Emery-Wallis 1979; Lickorish 1979; Montagu 1979), a factor which was becoming increasingly clear to policy-makers and tourist authorities. The recent study by Myerscough (1988) endorses this. In fact the major growth in museum provision during the 1970s and 1980s was in the independent sector, drawing much on the tourist and leisure market for its support.

For the Association, inflation was taking its toll. Subscriptions were raised in 1976 with minor adjustments the following year and again in 1979. The Museum Assistants Group asked Council to look at the advantages and implications of relocating the Association's office outside London in 1976, although an advantageous rental currently obtained on the offices at 87 Charlotte Street. Concern at the burden of work on the Association's staff led the President to suggest (Tebble 1978) that a Director-General should be appointed to oversee and co-ordinate the complexities of the operation. The following year a Director, John Sheriff, was appointed, a decision bolstered by the offer of an annual grant of £10,000 for three years by the CUKT to contribute towards the cost. However, despite this, and the subscription increases of 1979, the Association was in deficit again at the end of that financial year. A further subscription increase the following year could not contain inflation and escalating staff costs; as a consequence the occupants of two posts, that of Director and Information Officer were made redundant. The Association's long cherished aim of a Royal Charter, work on which had again been proceeding, was yet again deferred until its financial situation had improved. Further change befell the Association in that planning permission for the use of 87 Charlotte Street as offices was withdrawn and in 1979 the headquarters was moved to 34 Bloomsbury Way.

The Museum Documentation Association

After some nine years of development with the aid of grants from DES and the British Library Research and Development fund, IRGMA – the Association's information retrieval group – launched a series of record cards to facilitate collection documentation. These could be used in a traditional card index or file but were structured to provide an input document for those wishing to computerize their records using the programs now developed. Over 250,000 of these cards were sold in the financial year 1976–77 to some 160 institutions. Clearly the Association could not continue to administer this without additional resources. But there was also the question of the development and maintenance of the system and the need for an advisory service as well. Following discussions with the Standing Commission, the Area Museum Councils and the national museums, sufficient financial support was promised to set up an independent organization – the Museum Documentation Association (MDA) – to take over this work.

Museum training and ethics

Another issue of concern to the Association was its education programme. In February 1976 a 'think-tank' on its future development was held and a number of proposals made which would influence future planning of the work. However, because of the increase in the number of Diploma courses required and the higher costs involved, it became increasingly difficult for the Association to find museums willing to host them. In 1979 negotiations with the Department of Museum Studies at the University of Leicester led to the transfer of all compulsory Diploma Courses there from October 1980. This arrangement continued until the follow-up to the Hale Report (1987) when it became clear that government funding would be available for a scheme of professional training overseen by the industry itself. Accordingly the Association set up an independent Museum Training Institute in 1989 which it is expected will play a leading role in the development of training for all kinds of museum employee.

The annual meeting of 1977 saw the approval of a code of practice for museum authorities and guidelines for professional conduct (Boylan 1977).

The Museum Professionals Group, which had been responsible for the original impetus concerning professional conduct, called a meeting to discuss and further the work (Museum Professionals Group 1981). The Association subsequently developed its code of conduct for museum curators. This and a revised code of practice for museum authorities were both adopted by the annual meeting in 1987 and are published in the *Museums Yearbook*. The previous year the Association created an Ethics Panel with Dr A J Duggan as chairman.

The Drew Report

In January 1979 the Drew Report was published. This was the report of a working party set up by the Standing Commission (1979) to continue work on the designation of provincial centres of excellence and to produce a preliminary plan for a national system of museum services as envisaged in the Wright Report. This proposed *inter alia* that a small number of museums with excellent collections and serving a wide area should be designated to receive a government grant for both running costs and capital schemes; that certain museums with specialized collections of more than local area interest might be eligible for one-time direct grant-aid for approved capital expenditure; that county-wide museum consultative committees should be formed representing all museum interests to keep the museum facilities of the county under review and to make recommendations regarding the grant-aiding of projects to the Area Museum Councils. Subsequently the development of these committees was reviewed by a working party (Museums and Galleries Commission 1982). On the question of a central policy-making body, it was proposed that this be set up in two sections: the first as a Commission similar to the Standing Commission; the second a representative museums council which would report to the Commission. The first of these can be considered to be the reorganization of the Standing Commission into the Museums and Galleries Commission with new terms of reference, reported by Sir Arthur Drew (1981) to the Manchester conference. Thus another of the Association's long declared objectives came rather closer to fruition.

The Association today

In 1983, the Council, concerned at the marginal financial situation that had plagued the Association for so long, engaged consultants to examine its operation. This report recommended major changes and the appointment of a Director-General to oversee them. Council, after considerable debate, accepted the report and disestablished the post of Secretary, thus making Brenda Capstick redundant. Major changes were then introduced into the administration of the Association and into the development of services to members. A number of marketing initiatives were introduced to generate income. John Fox was in due course appointed as Director-General but took early retirement in 1986; he was replaced by Graeme Farnell, previously Director of the Scottish Museums Council.

The most recent years of the Association lack historical perspective. They closely follow the strategies adopted by Council in 1983. Among them the publication of the *Manual of Curatorship*, jointly published with Butterworths in 1984 with a revised edition two years later, and the Museum Data-Base Project which made available detailed information of the museums of the UK and their operation which had previously been inaccessible. Both projects were funded by the Office of Arts and Libraries. In addition the Council created a subsidiary company, Museum Enterprises Ltd, the profits from which are used for the benefit of the Association. This change of course suggests a further watershed and the point where a new chapter, yet to be written, should commence. In the meantime the Association celebrates its centenary with a nation-wide Museums Year in 1989.

NOTES

1 The following attended the meeting in York on 3 May 1888: R Cameron (Sunderland Museum); J W Carr (Nottingham University Museum); Revd W C Hey (Yorkshire Philosophical Society); E Howarth (Sheffield Museum and Art Gallery); C Madeley (Warrington Library and Museum); W W Midgley (Bolton Museum); T J Moore (Liverpool Museum); S W North (Vice-President, Yorkshire Philosophical Society); H M Platnauer (Yorkshire Philosophical Society Museum); C G Virgo (Queen's Park Museum, Manchester); Butler Wood (Bradford Museum).

2 The eleven museums and their delegates represented at the York meeting on 20 June 1889 were Bolton: W W Midgley; Bradford: B Wood; Brighton: B Lomax; Liverpool: The Revd H H Higgins; Northampton: F J George; Nottingham: J W Carr; Scarborough: J H Phillips; Sheffield: E Howarth; Stockport: Alderman H Turner & J Tym; Sunderland: J M E Bowley & R Cameron; York: The Revd W C Hey, S W North & H M Platnauer.

3 The new Council comprised the President, Secretaries and the members of the old organizing committee with the following additions: Professor W Boyd Dawkins (Curator of the Manchester Museum, Owen's College); J Paton (Superintendent of the Kelvingrove Museum, Glasgow); F W Rudler (Curator of the Museum of Practical Geology, London); Dr R T Scharff (Keeper of the Natural History Division of the National Museum of Science and Art, Dublin). The post of Treasurer was filled by Alderman W H Brittain (Chairman of the Free Public Library and Museum Committee, Sheffield). It is assumed that Professor Boyd Dawkins and Mr S W North filled the positions of Vice-President, although this is not stated in the report or minutes of the Liverpool meeting.

4 The Association's Committee on Labelling reported in *Proc Mus Ass* 1891 and 1892. Other references of this period either directly or indirectly applicable to labelling include: Bolton (1892;1894;1896); Miers (1897); Jackson (1899); Bather (1900); Lucas (1901); Anon (1901); Lowe (1904).

5 While the Editorial in the *Museums J* 17, 49 carries overtones of intrigue, it is generous in its announcement of the Sheffield meeting. However, the comments on the report of the meeting are ungenerous (*Museums J* 18, 85).

6 The Chairman of the Committee was Professor J A Green of Sheffield University and the Vice-Chairman Dr F A Bather (British Museum (Natural History)). H Bolton (Bristol Museum) and Dr J A Clubb (Liverpool Museum) acted as Secretaries. The Committee's membership fluctuated and had increased slightly by the time of the final report; it included a number of Museums Association members.

7 The presidential badge was designed by R A Ray, ARCA, Principal, Sunderland School of Art. The badge is in silver gilt a Greek cross on an annular border bearing the words: MUSEUMS ASSOCIATION FOUNDED 1889. The border is broken by the cross terminals each of which has a mineral mounted in a circular panel representing England (garnet), Ireland (Connemara marble), Scotland (Cairngorm) and Wales (gold nugget). These also represent geology. Superimposed underneath the cross is the square centrepiece of Limoges enamel, the four corners containing symbols representing the chief subject areas of museum collections: flora (an Arum Lily); fauna (a beaver); art (palette and brushes); archaeology (a stone circle). In the centre of the cross is the lamp of learning. On the reverse of the badge is the inscription: THIS INSIGNA OF THE PRESIDENT IS THE GIFT OF JAMES DOWNS, OBE, JP, OF HULL. DECEMBER 1926.

8 The members of the Royal Commission on National Museums and Galleries were: The Rt Hon the Viscount D'Abernon (Chairman); The Hon Evan Charteris; Sir Martin Conway; Dr A E Cowley; Sir Lionel Earle; Sir Richard Glazebrook; Sir Thomas Heath; Sir George MacDonald; Sir Henry Miers; Col Sir Courtauld Thomson; Sir Robert Witt.

9 The following members gave evidence to the Royal Commission for the Museums Association: Sir Francis G Ogilvie (President); Dr Herbert Bolton (Bristol); Dr Ernest Lowe (Leicester); Mr Tom Sheppard (Hull); Dr James Simpson (Liverpool).

10 Sir Henry Miers had served on the following committees: British Association Committee on Museums in Relation to Education; Ministry of Reconstruction Adult Education Committee; the Royal Commission on National Museums and Galleries.

11 It should be noted that Sir Henry Miers included art museums but not art galleries in his survey. This means that statistics and tables include the Manchester City Art Gallery and the Victoria and Albert Museum but not the Walker Art Gallery, Liverpool or the National Gallery. This fine distinction appears to be based on whether or not the gallery or museum collects decorative art material.

12 The Sub-Committee on Training Course and Diplomas, subsequently renamed Sub-Committee on Education comprised the following members: Dr Cyril Fox (National Museum of Wales) - Chairman; W A Smallcombe (Reading) – Secretary; W A Gunn (Newport); Dr Ernest Lowe (Leicester); Professor L P W Renouf (University Museum, Cork); Alderman Charles Squires (Leicester); Dr William E Swinton (British Museum (Natural History)).

13 The Sub-Committee on Post-war Reconstruction of Museums and Art Galleries formed by Council on 14 November 1941 comprised: Major S F Markham (President); Sir Eric Maclagan; Dr D A Allan and Mr Christopher F C Hawkes.

14 The deputation from the Association that met representatives of the Ministry of Reconstruction, the Board of Education and the Treasury in March 1943 comprised: Dr D A Allen (President); Mr S D Cleveland; Sir Cyril Fox; Dr M B Hodge; Sir Eric Maclagan; Major S F Markham and Dr F S Wallis.

15 The first members of the ICOM National Committee were: Mr Frank Lambert (Chairman); Sir John Forsdyke; Sir Clive Forster-Cooper; Dr Herman Shaw; Mr Trenchard Cox; Sir Cyril Fox; Dr Douglas Allan; Mr Leigh Ashton.

16 The delegation to the first meeting of ICOM in Paris comprised: Dr D A Allan; Sir Leigh Ashton; Mr G L Conran; Mr Trenchard Cox; Mr W Currall; Mr F C Francis (representing Sir John Forsdyke); Mrs M Harrison; Mr A E Popham; Dr H Shaw; Mr D Sutton; Dr G M Vevers and Dr A Wittlin. Mr Philip Hendy attended a session on the restoration of paintings.

17 The members of the Department of Education and Science Committee on Provincial Museums and Galleries were: Mr C W Wright (Chairman); Mr F Atkinson; Miss M E Burkett; Mr D T-D Clarke; Mr I M Evans; Mr D L A Farr; Dr S M K Henderson; Alderman C J Peers; the Earl of Plymouth; Sir John Pope-Hennessy; the Earl of Rosse; Mr G J Spence; Alderman F J Stott; Alderman R A Whittingham; Sir John Wolfenden. Mr R B K Stevenson replaced Dr Henderson in May 1972.

The illustrations, which are mainly from contemporary sources, are gratefully acknowledged to the Museums Association, National Museums and Galleries on Merseyside, Sheffield Weekly News and the South Yorkshire Notes and Queries.

BIBLIOGRAPHY

ACADEMICUS (1880) 'A museum conference', letter in *Nature* 21, 492

ALLAN, D A (1943) 'Museums reorganization: a long-term plan' *Museums J* 43, 65-73

ALLAN, D A (1945) 'Museums manpower' *Museums J* 45, 73-80

ALLEN, J Romilly (1880a) 'A museum conference', letter in *Nature* 17, 468

ALLEN, J Romilly (1880b) 'A museum conference', letter in *Nature* 17, 515

ANON (1901) 'A museum label', *Museums J* 1, 24-5

ANON (1919) 'Museum, education, and the Board', *Nature* 104, 114-15

ATKINSON, F (1968) 'Regional museums', *Museums J* 68, 74-77

BAILEY, J (1922) 'The case for a Royal Commission on Museums', *Museums J* 22, 89-95

BAILEY, J (1926) 'The Carnegie Trustees and provincial museums', *Museums J* 26, 31-36

BAILEY, J (1927) 'London museums and the taxpayer', *Museums J* 27, 238-40

BAILEY, J (1928a) 'Sir Henry Miers' Report on the public museums of the British Isles', *Museums J* 27, 370-77

BAILEY, J (1928b) 'Discussion on Sir Henry Miers' Report to the Carnegie Trustees. I. Finance', *Museums J* 28, 123-28

BALFOUR, H (1912) 'A national folk museum', *Museums J* 11, 221-225

BARTON, K (1974) 'Rescuing museums' in Rahtz, P A (Ed) *Rescue Archaeology*, Penguin Books, Harmondsworth

BASSETT, D A (1982) *The making of a National Museum*, Honourable Society of Cymmrodorion

BATHER, F A (1900) 'Exhibition labels for Blastoidea', *Proc Mus Ass* 1900, 94-115

BATHER, F A (1903) 'Dr Meyer on some European Museums', *Museums J* 11, 319-29

BATHER, F A (1907) 'Interchangeability in cases', *Museums J* 6, 330-35

BATHER, F A (1910) 'Business devices for the curator', *Museums J* 9, 257-81

BATHER, F A (1915) 'Museums and the war', *Museums J* 15, 2-10

BATHER, F A (1928) 'Discussion on Sir Henry Miers' Report to the Carnegie Trustees. I. Research in the smaller museums', *Museums J* 28, 153-56

BATHER, F A (1929) 'La vie des associations: The Museums Association', *Mouseion* 8, 157-70

BESTERMAN, T and BOTT, V (1982) 'To pay or not to pay', *Museums J* 82, 118-1

BLEDISLOE, Viscount (1939) 'Museums: their past, present and future', *Museums J* 39, 214-29

BOARD OF EDUCATION (1931) *Memorandum on the Possibility of Increased Co-operation between Public Museums and Public Educational Institutions*, HMSO, London

BOLTON, H (1892) 'A catalogue of types and figured specimens.. in the Geological Department of the Manchester Museum, Owen's College', *Proc Mus Ass* 1892, 96-129

BOLTON, H (1894) 'Supplementary list of type fossils in the Manchester Museum', *Proc Mus Ass* 1894, 250-254

BOLTON, H (1896) 'Descriptive geological labels', *Proc Mus Ass* 1896, 69-91

BOLTON, H (1898) 'Provincial museums and the Museums Association', *Proc Mus Ass* 1898, 89-93

BOLTON, H (1906) 'The future of museums', *Museums J* 5, 251-56

BOLTON, H (1924) 'Presidential Address', *Museums J* 24, 25-39; 50-54; 90-101

BOLTON, H (1928) 'Discussion on Sir Henry Miers' Report to the Carnegie Trustees. II. Museum planning; III. Workrooms and storage; IV. Staff', *Museums J* 28, 182-89

BOYLAN, P J (1977) 'Museum ethics: Museums Association policies', *Museums J* 77, 106-11

BRITISH ASSOCIATION (1887) 'Report of the Committee on the Provincial Museums of the United Kingdom', *Report of the British Association for the Advancement of Science*, 1887, 97-130

BRITISH ASSOCIATION (1888) 'A further report of the Committee on the Provincial Museums of the United Kingdom', *Report of the British Association for the Advancement of Science*, 1888, 124-132

BRITISH ASSOCIATION (1920) 'Final report of the Committee on Museums in Relation to Education', *Report of the British Association for the Advancement of Science*, 1920, 267-280

BRITISH MUSEUM (1939) *Air Raid Precautions in museums, picture galleries and libraries*, Trustees of the British Museum, London

BULLARD, C (1974) 'The Daphne Bullard Trust', *Museums J* 73, 166

CARLISLE, Esmé [Countess of] (1987) *A History of the Commission*, Museums and Galleries Commission, London

CARPENTER, G H (1929) 'Discussion on Sir Henry Miers' Report to the Carnegie Trustees. VI. Co-operation between local museums', *Museums J* 28, 247-53

CARTER, C (1970) 'Then and now: professional ruminations after forty-five years', *Museums J* 69, 161-63

CHEETHAM, F W (1966) 'Towards a national museum service?', *Museums J* 66, 167-74

CHEETHAM, F W (1968) 'A national museum service for Britain', *Museums J* 68, 70-73

CHEETHAM, F W (1974) 'Local government reorganization and the Norfolk Museums Service', *Museums J* 74, 27-28

CHUBB, E C (1929) 'The museums and galleries of South Africa', *Museums J* 28, 216-22

CLARKE, D T-D (1969) 'Register of museums', *Museums J* 69, 141

CLEVELAND, S D (1951) 'Association reflections', *Museums J* 51, 83-90

COATES, H & RODGER, A M (1905) 'School children and museums, Part II', *Museums J* 4, 217-19

COMMITTEE ON RETRENCHMENT (1916) 'Retrenchment Committee's explanation', *Museums J* 15, 292-93

CONRAN, G L (1961) 'Boom in museums', *Museums J* 60, 271-72

COTTESLOE, LORD (1964) *Report of the Committee of Enquiry into the Sale of Works of Art by Public Bodies*, HMSO, London

COWPER, L I (1935) 'British military museums', *Museums Journal* 35, 40-49

CROWTHER, H (1929) 'Discussion on Sir Henry Miers' Report to the Carnegie Trustees. V. The Leeds Museum and schools', *Museums J* 28, 221-25

DAVIES, S (1985) *By the Gains of Industry: Birmingham Museums and Art Gallery 1885-1985*, Birmingham

DAWKINS, W Boyd (1876) Address at the Manchester Literary and Philosophical Society, noted in *Nature* 15, 129

DAWKINS, W Boyd (1877) 'The need of museum reform', *Nature* 16, 78-79

DEAS, J A Charlton (1911) 'National art loans: a plea from the provinces', *Museums J* 11, 2

DEPARTMENT OF EDUCATION AND SCIENCE (1971) *Museums in Education*, Education Survey 12, DES, HMSO, London

DEPARTMENT OF EDUCATION AND SCIENCE (1973) *Provincial Museums and Galleries: a report of a Committee appointed by the Paymaster General*, DES, HMSO, London

DIBDIN, E Rimbault (1922) 'The organisation of picture exhibitions in the provinces', *Museums J* 22, 96-102; 112-16

DREW, A [Sir] (1981) 'The government and museums', *Museums J* 81 (supplement), 3-5

ECCLES, [Viscount] (1973) 'The report of the Committee on Provincial Museums and Galleries', *Museums J* 73, 120-24

EDWARDS, J (1965) 'Local authority museums and the Public Libraries and Museums Act, 1964', *Museums J* 65, 6-11

EMERY-WALLIS, F A J (1979) 'The value of museums to the economy', *Museums J* 79, 115-16

EWERT, J C *et al* (1909) Letter addressed to *The Times*, April 1909, published in *Museums J* 8, 386-92

FLOWER, W H (1876) 'Museum specimens for teaching purposes', *Nature* 15, 144-46; 184-86; 204-06

FLOWER, W H (1898) *Essay on Museums and Other Subjects Connected with Natural History*, Books for Libraries Press, New York, 1972 (reprint)

FORD, W K (1955) 'Notes on the earlier history of the City of Liverpool Public Museums', *Liverpool Libraries, Museums & Arts Committee Bulletin*, 5 (1&2), 3-15

FORSDYKE, E J (1941) 'The Museum in war time', *British Museum Quarterly* 15, 4

FOUNDOUKIDIS, E (1945) *Cultural reconstruction*, International Museums Office, Paris

FOX, A LANE (1878) 'The arrangement of museums', letter in *Nature* 17, 484-85

GOODE, G Brown (1895) 'The principles of museum administration', *Proc Mus Ass* 1895, 69-148; also *Annual Report of the Smithsonian Institution*, 1897, 193

GREEN, J A (1915) 'Discussion on museums in relation to education at the London Conference, 1915', *Museums J* 15, 129-45

GREENWOOD, T (1888) *Museums and Art Galleries*, Simpkin, Marshall and Co, London

GRIGGS, G P (1953) 'Saving the national treasures', *Museums J*, 52, 237-39

GÜNTHER, A C L G (1880) 'Museums, their use and improvement', *Nature* 22, 393-97

HALLETT, C (1913) 'The work of a guide demonstrator', *Museums J* 13, 192-202

HARDEN, D B (1948) 'Recruitment and training for the museum service', *Museums J* 48, 1-5

HARDEN, D B (1956) 'Museum development in Great Britain', *Museums J* 56, 161-65

HARDEN, D B (1961) 'The museum service – past present and future', *Museums J* 61, 92-99

HARRISON, R (1971) 'The first seven years 1963-70: reflections on the work of Area Councils', *Museums J* 71, 20-24

HEBDITCH, M G (1974) 'The museum as a firm', *Museums J* 74, 45-46

HERDMAN, W A (1887) 'An ideal natural history museum', address to the Literary and Philosophical Society of Liverpool, 21 March 1887, in Greenwood, T *Museums and Art Galleries*, 180-95, Simpkin, Marshall and Co, London, 1888

HICKS, [The Revd Canon] (1892) 'Local museums of art and history', *Proc Mus Ass* 1892, 46-50

HIGGINS, H H (1885) 'Museums of natural history', address to the Literary and Philosophical Society of Liverpool noted in *Nature* 31, 564

HILL, F [Sir] (1970) 'The Redcliffe-Maud Report', *Museums J* 70, 105-106

HODGE, M B (1947) 'The problem of the small town museum', *Museums J* 47, 161-65

HODGE, M B (1949) 'Museum co-operation: 2. The part of the provincial museum', *Museums J* 49, 158-61

HOLMES, E M (1880) 'Museum conference', letter in *Nature* 22, 10

HORWOOD, A R (1913) 'The school and the museum', *Report of the British Association for the Advancement of Science*, 1913, 743-44

HOWARTH, E (1877) 'Museums', *Nature* 15, 276

HOWARTH, E (1880) 'A museum conference', letter in *Nature* 21, 492

HOWARTH, E (1891) 'On some recent museum legislation', *Proc Mus Ass* 1891, 121-126

HOWARTH, E [Ed] (1918) *The Educational Value of Museums & the Formation of Local War Museums: Report of Proceedings*, W Wesley & Son, London

HOWARTH, E and PLATNAUER, H M [Comp](1911) *Directory of Museums in Great Britain and Ireland together with a section on Indian and Colonial Museums*, Museums Association

HOWARTH, W *et al* (1923) 'Report of the Joint Committee . . . on the question of how far the system of circulating objects from the Victoria and Albert Museum meets the needs of the provinces', *Museums J* 22, 163-64

HOYLE, W E (1891) 'The registration and cataloguing of museum specimens', *Proc Mus Ass* 1891, 59-70

HOYLE, W E (1898) 'The electric light installation in the Manchester Museum', *Proc Mus Ass* 1898, 95-105

HOYLE, W E (1901) 'Some useful applications of card catalogues', *Museums J* 1, 297-305

HOYLE, W E (1903) 'The use of museums in teaching', *Museums J* 2, 229-39

HOYLE, W E (1906) 'The education of a curator', *Museums J* 6, 4-24

HOYLE, W E (1920) Letter to Lord Sudeley, 15 November 1920 [Sudeley Papers, Museums Association]

HOYLE, W E (1921) 'Training and Diplomas for museum curators', *Museums J* 20, 173-80

HOYLE, W E and BOLTON, H (1894) 'Classified cataloguing as applied to Palaeozoic fossils', *Proc Mus Ass* 1894, 167-179

HUDSON, K (1965) 'The taming of industrial archaeology', *Museums J* 65, 36-41

HYSLOP, A B (1930) 'The Museum policy of the Carnegie Trustees', *Museums J* 30, 125-29

JACKSON, R T (1899) 'Ink and paper for museum labels', *Proc Mus Ass* 1899, 77-79; also *Proc American Ass for the Advancement of Science* 47 (1898), 378-379

JACOB, J (1971) 'The sale and disposal of museum objects: the principles involved and an account of some cases in point', *Museums J* 71, 112-15

JAMES, P (1962) 'Editorial – Area Councils', *Museums J*, 61, 231-32

JOHNSTON, E (1970) 'Resolution on museum admission charges', *Museums J*, 71, 123-24

KAVANAGH, G (1984) 'Museum, memorials and Minenwerfers', *Museums J*, 84, 65-70

KELLY, T (1977) *A History of Public Libraries in Great Britain 1845-1975*, Library Association, London

KENNEDY, H A (1938) *Local Museums: Notes on their Building and Conduct*, Museums Association, London

KOETSCHAU, K (1903) 'Museumwesen und Kunstförderung', in *Jahrbuch der Bildenden Kunst, 1903*, 93-98, Deutsche Jahrbuch-gesellschaft, Berlin

LEE, A H (1928) 'A museum summer school', *Museums J* 28, 50-52

LENEY, F (1909) 'The Norwich Museums Association', *Museums J* 8, 227-37

LEONARD, J H (1914) 'A museum guide and his work', *Museums J* 13, 234-46

LEWIS, G (1969) 'Must museums be within walls? Museums and environmental interpretation', *Museums J* 69, 116-18

LEWIS, G (1983) 'The training of museum personnel in the United Kingdom', *Museums J* 83, 65-70

LEWIS, G *et al* (1967) 'Information retrieval for museums', *Museums J* 67, 88-120

LICKORISH, L J (1979) 'The value of museums to the economy', *Museums J* 79, 117-18

LOUGHBROUGH, B (1978) 'The effects of local government reorganization', *Museums J* 77, 165-66

LOWE, E E (1903) 'The registration and numeration of museum specimens' *Museums J* 3, 258-66

LOWE, E E (1904) Letter of 2 September 1904 to Editor, *Museums J* 4, 106

LOWE, E E (1918) Letter to the President, Board of Trade, 16 January 1918 [Sudeley Papers, Museums Association]

LOWE, E E (1920a) 'The transfer of museums to the Education Authorities' *Museums J* 19, 105-11

LOWE, E E (1920b) 'The Public Libraries Act 1919 and its effect on the future policy of museums' *Museums J* 20, 83-89

LOWE, E E (1928a) 'Notes on American museums' *Museums J* 27, 208-17; 238-46
LOWE, E E (1928b) *A Report on American Museum Work*, Carnegie United Kingdom Trust, Dumfermline
LUCAS, F A (1901) 'Some American labels', *Museums J* 1, 77-79

MADELEY, C (1904) 'District museums: a suggestion to county councils', *Museums J* 4, 117-21
MARKHAM, S F (1938) *The Museums and Art Galleries of the British Isles*, Carnegie United Kingdom Trust, Dumfermline
MARKHAM, S F (1948) *Directory of Museums and Art Galleries of the British Isles*, Museums Association, London
MARKHAM, S F and HARGREAVES, H (1936) *The Museums of India*, Museums Association, London
MARKHAM, S F and OLIVER, W R B (1934) *A Report on the Museums and Art Galleries of New Zealand*, Museums Association, London
MARKHAM, S F and RICHARDS, H C (1934a) *A Report on the Museums and Art Galleries of Australia*, Museums Association, London
MARKHAM, S F and RICHARDS, H C (1934b) *A Directory of Museums and Art Galleries in Australia and New Zealand*, Museums Association, London
MEYER, A B (1877) 'Museum reform', letter in *Nature* 16, 227
MEYER, A B (1903) 'K Koetschau on museums in 1902', *Museums Journal* 2, 363-64
MIERS, H A (1897) 'On the arrangement of the mineral collection in the University Museum, Oxford', *Proc Mus Ass* 1897, 37-46
MIERS, H A [Sir] (1928) *A Report on the Public Museums of the British Isles (Other than the National Museums)*, Carnegie United Kingdom Trust, Dumfermline
MIERS, H A [Sir] (1929) 'Co-operation: the task of the Association', *Museums J* 29, 33-56
MIERS, H A [Sir] (1930) 'Address by the President', *Museums J* 30, 33-44
MIERS, H A [Sir] (1931) 'Address by the President', *Museums J* 31, 173-86
MIERS, H A [Sir] (1932) 'Address by the President', *Museums J* 32, 129-44
MIERS, H A [Sir] and MARKHAM, S F (1932a) *Directory of Museums and Art Galleries in Canada, Newfoundland, Bermuda, the British West Indies, British Guiana and the Faulkland Islands*, Museums Association, London
MIERS, H A [Sir] and MARKHAM, S F (1932b) *Report on the Museums of Canada*, Museums Association, London
MIERS, H A [Sir] and MARKHAM, S F (1933a) *Directory of Museums and Art Galleries in British Africa, Malta, Cyprus and Gibraltar*, Museums Association, London
MIERS, H A [Sir] and MARKHAM, S F (1933b) *Report on the Museums and Art Galleries in British Africa together with a Report on the Museums of Malta, Cyprus and Gibraltar*, Museums Association, London
MIERS, H A [Sir] and MARKHAM, S F (1937) 'Final report to the Carnegie Corporation of New York on the activities of the Empire Grants Committee', *Museums J* 37, 77-92
MILLER, E (1973) *That Noble Cabinet: a History of the British Museum*, André Deutsch, London
MINISTRY OF RECONSTRUCTION (1919a) *Adult Education Committee: Interim Report: Libraries and Museums*, HMSO, London
MINISTRY OF RECONSTRUCTION (1919b) *Adult Education Committee: Final Report*, HMSO, London

MINTO, J (1906) 'The relation of provincial museums to national institutions', *Museums J* 5, 219-24

MITCHELL, J M (1932) 'The museum policy of the Carnegie Trustees', *Museums J* 31, 491-96

MONTAGU OF BEAULIEU, [Lord] (1979) 'Enterprise in museums', *Museums J* 79, 118-19

MORTON, G H (1894) 'Museums of the past, the present and the future, particularly those of Liverpool', *Proc Liverpool Naturalists Field Club*, 1894

MOSLEY, C (1932) 'Curators' salaries – cuts'. Letter to the Editor. *Museums J* 32, 256

MOSLEY, S L (1906) 'Museums and private collections', *Museums J* 5, 257-59

MURRAY, D (1904) *Museums: Their History and Use*, Vols 1-3, James MacLehose and Sons, Glasgow

MUSEUM PROFESSIONALS GROUP (1981) 'Towards a code of ethics in museums', *Museum Professionals Group Transactions*, 16

MUSEUM PROFESSIONALS GROUP (1985) 'Admission charges at national museums', *Museum Professionals Group Transactions*, 21

MUSEUMS AND GALLERIES COMMISSION (1982) *Countywide Consultative Committees for Museums*, HMSO, London

MUSEUMS AND GALLERIES COMMISSION (1984) *Review of the Area Museum Councils and Services*, HMSO, London

MUSEUMS AND GALLERIES COMMISSION (1986) *Museums in Scotland*, HMSO, London

MUSEUMS AND GALLERIES COMMISSION (1987) *Museum Professional Training and Career Structure*, HMSO, London

MUSEUMS AND GALLERIES COMMISSION (1988) *The National Museums: the National Museums and Galleries of the United Kingdom*, HMSO, London

MUSEUMS ASSOCIATION (1903a) 'Voluntary help in museums', *Museums J* 2, 255-57

MUSEUMS ASSOCIATION (1903b) 'Lectures in museums', *Museums J* 2, 287-88

MUSEUMS ASSOCIATION (1905) 'Library and museum rating', *Museums J* 5, 156-61

MUSEUMS ASSOCIATION (1916) 'Deputation to the Prime Minister on the closing of museums', *Museums J* 15, 317-39

MUSEUMS ASSOCIATION (1922) 'Museums and the Geddes Axe', *Museums J* 21, 203-4

MUSEUMS ASSOCIATION (1925) 'Beating the great drum', *Museums J* 24, 175-7

MUSEUMS ASSOCIATION (1927a) 'Royal Commission on Museums', *Museums J* 27, 53-55

MUSEUMS ASSOCIATION (1927b) 'The Executive Committee and the Royal Commission on National Museums and Galleries', *Museums J* 27, 53-55

MUSEUMS ASSOCIATION (1928) 'Royal Commission on National Museums and Galleries', *Museums J* 28, 117-18

MUSEUMS ASSOCIATION (1929a) 'The co-ordination of museums', *Museums J* 29, 145-47

MUSEUMS ASSOCIATION (1929b) 'Home museums and the Dominions', *Museums J* 29, 213-15

MUSEUMS ASSOCIATION (1930a) 'The training of the curator', *Museums J* 29, 293-96

MUSEUMS ASSOCIATION (1930b) 'Proposals of the Carnegie Trustees', *Museums J* 29, 333-34

MUSEUMS ASSOCIATION (1930c) 'Open-air folk museums', *Museums J* 29, 377-81

MUSEUMS ASSOCIATION (1930d) 'Applications for grants from the Carnegie Trustees', *Museums J* 30, 125

MUSEUMS ASSOCIATION (1930e) 'The short training course for curators', *Museums J* 30, 180-83

MUSEUMS ASSOCIATION (1931a) 'Folk Museum Committee', *Museums J* 30, 300

MUSEUMS ASSOCIATION (1931b) 'The partition of Hertfordshire for museum work', *Museums J* 30, 361-62

MUSEUMS ASSOCIATION (1931c) 'The Standing Commission on Museums', *Museums J* 31, 5-6

MUSEUMS ASSOCIATION (1932a) 'Museums and the schools' *Museums J* 31, 485-87

MUSEUMS ASSOCIATION (1932b) 'Correspondence between the Museums Association and the Standing Commission on National [sic] Museums & Galleries on co-operation between national and provincial museums' *Museums J* 32, 144-47

MUSEUMS ASSOCIATION (1932c) 'Museums Association: Regulations governing the award of the Diploma of the Association', *Museums J* 32, 273-76

MUSEUMS ASSOCIATION (1934a) 'A great opportunity', *Museums J* 33, 421-22

MUSEUMS ASSOCIATION (1934b) 'Carnegie grants to museums: new policy', *Museums J* 34, 422-43

MUSEUMS ASSOCIATION (1934c) 'Grants to colonial museums: draft conditions', *Museums J* 34, 424

MUSEUMS ASSOCIATION (1936a) 'Carnegie Trustees' museum policy, 1936-40', *Museums J* 35, 405-408

MUSEUMS ASSOCIATION (1936b) 'The Carnegie Corporation and Australian and New Zealand museums', *Museums J* 36, 54-55

MUSEUMS ASSOCIATION (1938) 'National and provincial museums: scheme for extended advisory service', *Museums J* 37, 493-97

MUSEUMS ASSOCIATION (1939) 'Junior museum officials; inaugural meeting of new group', *Museums J* 39, 189-90

MUSEUMS ASSOCIATION (1940a) 'The proposed Commission on Museums', *Museums J* 39, 483-84

MUSEUMS ASSOCIATION (1940b) 'Grants for educational services by museums', *Museums J* 40, 11

MUSEUMS ASSOCIATION (1940c) 'Ministry of Information exhibitions', *Museums J* 40, 122-23

MUSEUMS ASSOCIATION (1942a) 'Post-war reconstruction of museums and art galleries', *Museums J* 42, 77

MUSEUMS ASSOCIATION (1942b) 'Memorandum on museums and reconstruction', *Museums J* 42, 78-80

MUSEUMS ASSOCIATION (1943) 'Post-war reconstruction: memorandum on local museum and art gallery planning', *Museums J* 43, 129

MUSEUMS ASSOCIATION (1945a) 'Museums and Art Galleries: a national service', *Museums J* 45, 33-45

MUSEUMS ASSOCIATION (1945b) 'The International Museums Office', *Museums J* 45, 149-51

MUSEUMS ASSOCIATION (1948) 'International Council of Museums: Paris conference', *Museums J* 48, 148

MUSEUMS ASSOCIATION (1954) 'Rating Committee', *Museums J* 54, 190-3

MUSEUMS ASSOCIATION (1963) 'Editorial', *Museums J* 62, 231-2

MUSEUMS ASSOCIATION (1968) 'Statement of Policy by the Museums Association Council on Local Government Reform', *Museums J* 68, 92

MUSEUMS ASSOCIATION (1971a) *Museums in Education*, report of a working party, Museums Association, London

MUSEUMS ASSOCIATION (1971b) *A Museum Service for the Nation*, proposals submitted to the 1970 Conference by the Council of the Museums Association, London

MUSEUMS ASSOCIATION (1987) *Museums UK: the Findings of the Museums Data-Base Project*, Museums Association, London

MUSEUMS ASSOCIATION (1989) 'Code of Practice for Museum Authorities' and 'Code of Conduct for Museum Curators', in *Museums Yearbook*, Museums Association, London

MYERSCOUGH, J (1988) *The Economic Importance of the Arts in Britain*, Policy Studies Institute, London

NIGHTINGALE, M D (1957) 'Towards a regional museum service', *Museums J* 57, 49-50

NIGHTINGALE, M D (1960a) 'Appeal', *Museums J* 59, 251-52

NIGHTINGALE, M D (1960b) 'Making history', *Museums J* 59, 277-78

NORTH, F J (1953) 'Why museums, and wherefore the Museums Association?', *Museums J* 53, 95-104

NORTH, F J, DAVISON, C F, & SWINTON, W E (1941) *Geology in the Museum*, Museums Association, London

NORTHBOURNE, Lord (1924) 'The Sudeley Committee', letter to *The Times*, 5 February 1924, reprinted in *Museums J* 23, 230-31

NORTHBOURNE, Lord (1927) 'Museums and the public', letter to *The Times*, 7 January 1927, reprinted in *Museums J* 26, 220-21

OWEN, D E (1969) 'Presidential address', *Museums J* 69, 97-99

OWEN, D E (1970) 'Regionalisation of museums: what is a region?', *Museums J* 70, 25-26

PATON, J (1877) 'Museum reform', letter in *Nature* 16, 183

PATON, J (1880a) 'A museum conference', letter in *Nature* 17, 442

PATON, J (1880b) 'A museum conference', letter in *Nature* 17, 514-15

PATON, J (1894) 'The education of the museum curator', *Proc Mus Ass*, 1894, 95-105

PEACOCK, A and GODFREY, C (1974) 'The economics of museums and galleries', *Museums J* 74, 55-58

PETRIE, W M Flinders (1891) 'Classified cataloguing', letter in *Nature*, reprinted in *Proc Mus Ass*, 1891, 64-66

PETRIE, W M Flinders (1897a) 'A federal staff for museums', *Proc Mus Ass*, 1897, 74-79

PETRIE, W M Flinders (1897b) Letter of 26 August 1896 to W E Hoyle, in *Proc Mus Ass*, 1897, 110

PETRIE, W M Flinders (1900) 'A national repository for science and art', *Proc Mus Ass*, 1900, 89-93

PLATNAUER, H M (1901) 'To utilize specialists', *Museums J* 1, 63-65

PLENDERLEITH, H J (1933) *The Preservation of Antiquities*, Museums Association, London

PLENDERLEITH, H J (1937) *The Conservation of Prints, Drawings, and Manuscripts*, Museums Association, London

PYRAH, B J (1988) *The History of the Yorkshire Museum and its Geological Collections*, William Sessions Ltd, York

ROBERTS, D A *et al* (1980) 'The Museum Documentation Association', *Museums J* 80, 81-85

ROSSE, [Earl of] *et al* (1963) 'Symposium on the Survey of Provincial Museums and Galleries by the Standing Commission on Museums and Galleries', *Museums J* 63, 185-200

ROYAL COMMISSION ON NATIONAL MUSEUMS AND GALLERIES (1928a) *Interim Report*, HMSO, London

ROYAL COMMISSION ON NATIONAL MUSEUMS AND GALLERIES (1928b) *Oral Evidence, Memoranda and Appendices to the Interim Report*, HMSO, London

ROYAL COMMISSION ON NATIONAL MUSEUMS AND GALLERIES (1929a) *Final Report, Part 1: general Conclusions and Recommendations*, HMSO, London

ROYAL COMMISSION ON NATIONAL MUSEUMS AND GALLERIES (1929b) *Oral Evidence, Memoranda and Appendices to the Final Report*, HMSO, London

ROYAL COMMISSION ON NATIONAL MUSEUMS AND GALLERIES (1930) *Final Report, Part 2: Conclusions and Recommendations relating to Individual Institutions*, HMSO, London

RUDLER, F W (1877) 'Museum reform', letter in *Nature* 16, 140

SALVADOR DE MADARIAGA, H E Don (1940) 'Museums and world peace', *Museums J* 39, 409-11

SCRUTTON, H (1970) 'The views and actions of Council on the Redcliffe-Maud Report', *Museums J* 70, 107

SINGLETON, H R (1966) 'The Leicester course', *Museums J* 66, 135-138

SKINNER, H D (1916) 'Museums and the Empire', *Museums J* 16, 175-77

SMITH, A (1971) 'The Postgraduate Course in Gallery and Museum Studies, Department of Art History, University of Manchester', *Museums J* 71, 100-101

SPALDING, D A E (1966) 'The natural history department and distribution studies', *Museums J* 65, 292-95

STANDING COMMISSION ON MUSEUMS AND GALLERIES (1963) *Survey of Provincial Museums and Galleries*, HMSO, London [The Rosse Report]

STANDING COMMISSION ON MUSEUMS AND GALLERIES (1967) *Area Museum Services, 1963-1966*, HMSO, London

STANDING COMMISSION ON MUSEUMS AND GALLERIES (1968) *Universities and Museums*, HMSO, London

STANDING COMMISSION ON MUSEUMS AND GALLERIES (1971) *Report and Recommendations on the Preservation of Technological Material*, HMSO, London

STANDING COMMISSION ON MUSEUMS AND GALLERIES (1973) 'Loans from national institutions to provincial museums' in *Ninth Report 1960-1973*, HMSO, London

STANDING COMMISSION ON MUSEUMS AND GALLERIES (1977) *Report on University Museums*, HMSO, London

STANDING COMMISSION ON MUSEUMS AND GALLERIES (1979) *Framework for a System of Museums*, HMSO, London [The Drew Report]

STANDING COMMISSION ON MUSEUMS AND GALLERIES (1980) *Conservation*, HMSO, London

STANDING COMMISSION ON MUSEUMS AND GALLERIES (1981) *Report on Museums in Wales*, HMSO, London

STANSFIELD, G (1967) 'Museums in the countryside', *Museums J* 67, 212-18

STANSFIELD, G (1969) (Ed) 'Conference on countryside centres', *Museums J* 69, 63-73

STORRIE, F R (1970) 'The Wheatley Report', *Museums J* 70, 107-108

SUDELEY, Lord (1911) *The Public Utility of Museums*, T J S Guilford & Co, Kingston-on-Thames

SUDELEY, Lord (1915) Letter to CUKT dated 20 October 1915 and reply of 29 December 1915. [Sudeley Papers, Museums Association].

TAYLOR, A J P (1965) *English History 1914-1945*, Oxford University Press

TEBBLE, N (1978) 'Into the eighties: Presidential address', *Museums J* 78, 46-48

THOMPSON, J (1982) 'The accreditation scheme of the Museums Association 1974-82: a review', *Museums J* 71, 161-63

WALLIS, F S (1938) 'Delimitation of museum areas', *Museums J* 38, 182-83

WARHURST, A (1986) 'Triple crisis in University museums', *Museums J* 86, 137-140

WAVERLEY, Lord (1952) *The Export of Works of Art*, HMSO, London

WEBB, W M (1908) Letter to *The Times*, 11 July 1908, also printed in *Museums J* 8, 54-58

WHEELER, R E Mortimer [Sir] *et al* (1957) 'A regional museum service', *Museums J* 57, 109-20

WILKIE, J (1939) 'The Carnegie Trustees and the Markham Report', *Museums J* 39, 291-93

WILLETT, F (1986) 'The crisis in University museums in Scotland', *Museums J* 86, 141-144

WILLIAMS, A (1981) *A Heritage for Scotland: Scotland's National Museums and Galleries: the Next 25 Years*, Report of a Committee appointed by the Secretary of State for Scotland, HMSO, Glasgow

WINSTANLEY, B R (1940) 'The Derbyshire School Museum Service', *Museums J* 39, 473-78

WOOLNOUGH, F (1904) 'Museums and nature study', *Museums J* 4, 265-70

WRAY, L (1905) 'A system for the registration of the contents of museums', *Museums J* 4, 407-11

INDEX